TAMING
TENSION

By the Same Author

Africa's Wild Glory
Canada's Wild Glory
Splendour from the Land
Splendour from the Sea
Under Wilderness Skies
Under Desert Skies
Expendable
As a Tree Grows
Travels of the Tortoise
A Shepherd Looks at Psalm 23
Bold Under God
A Layman Looks at The Lord's Prayer
Rabboni
A Shepherd Looks at the
Good Shepherd and His Sheep
Mountain Splendour
Gideon—God's Giant

TAMING TENSION

W. Phillip Keller

BAKER BOOK HOUSE
Grand Rapids, Michigan

ISBN: 0-8010-5407-9

Library of Congress Catalog
Card Number: 77-94259

Printed in the United States of America

First Printing, June, 1979

Second Printing, October, 1979

To
Lynn and Rod
with
affection

123456

Contents

Before We Begin

There is perhaps no greater tyrant in the twentieth century than tension. Its tyranny is exerted upon every segment of society from the very aged down to the very young. So subtle and so unobtrusive are its devastating demands that few people are aware they they are living under its tyranny.

Yet, all over the world, there are innumerable broken lives, broken hearts, broken homes, broken bodies, and broken minds of men and women torn and tortured by tension.

For purposes of simplicity and clarity the term *tension* is used throughout this book to denote the whole gamut of evils which arise from and have their root in tension. These include stress in its multitudinous forms, pressures of all sorts, anxiety of every kind, fears both fancied and real, worry in its worst colors and just plain old-fashioned "fretting."

It is not my intention merely to analyze and examine this host of oppressive forces that fasten themselves on human beings with an iron hand. Nor do I wish to try to explain only how they come into operation and gradually victimize unsuspecting people. Rather I face the fact that they do and deal with the dilemma as it exists. It would be an absurdity of the first magnitude to pretend that one could or can live without tension. It has been demonstrated beyond any doubt that tension, to a degree, is absolutely essential to life, being an integral part of the total environment in which human beings must live.

What is here intended is simply to share with the reader a few simple secrets of how to understand and handle tension — how to tame it, how to meet its tyranny without being battered and broken by its belligerent abuse.

This is done in simple, straightforward layman's language. No attempt whatever is made to write in highly technical terminology or pretentious phraseology. Most of the material and ideas presented here are simple, practical, and, I hope, plain enough even for a child to understand and grasp and apply to his or her everyday life.

The thoughts and concepts included in this book have been distilled from half a century of learning to live under tension. My own nature and personality is such that I am readily susceptible to tension. It takes very little for me to become tense, worried, and fearful. In part this may be because of characteristics inherited from my forebears. My mother would often remark, "I'm not really worried—I'm just concerned!" which was a constant coverup for her own anxiety. My father, though seemingly a very successful man, died in his mid-fifties, killed, I am confident, by tension.

Added to this was a very unsettled childhood during which I was shunted about relentlessly from home to home with little or no sense of ever really "belonging" anywhere. Even worse, I often felt very unwanted, even despised. By the time I was twenty-five I had lived in seventeen different places — not one of which seemed really to be a true home. Consequently there crept into my makeup deep-rooted fears, anxieties, hostilities, and sensitivity to tension which only a lifetime of struggle and simple living have begun to bring under control.

The reader, then, will fully appreciate that this book has not been written in a theoretical manner from the lofty pedestal of a professional practitioner who hands out prescriptions to suffering patients. It is, rather, a sharing of practical measures which have proved effective in my own struggle to survive the tyranny of tension.

Again and again it has come home to me that were it not for the simple, basic, fundamental concepts contained in this book I would long ago have collapsed under the strain of twentieth-century living. Like a host of other human beings, I would have simply ended up a broken fragment of humanity cast up on the mounting scrap heap of society.

Unlike so many books nowadays which tend to specialize in some particular segment of human behavior, this one deals instead with the full orb of life. A human being is more than merely a mind or a body or a spirit which can be treated independently of the rest. A person in entirety and wholeness is body, mind, and spirit.

Because of this I have chosen deliberately to deal with all three areas of human life and human conduct. Tension in all of its various insidious forms brings pressure to bear upon every segment of our lives. What happens to the mind can affect the body and spirit; conversely, what influences the body or spirit can likewise make itself felt in the other two areas. We simply cannot separate ourselves into different compartments. Of necessity, of course, in order to be clear and simple, I have handled each separately in the full awareness that each contributes to the well-being of the other. A sound, healthy body is just as essential for a contented mind as a serene spirit is for a fit body.

I am aware that there are those who will contest this view. Others will deprecate it. Some will say that it is all too simple, too easy, too old-fashioned. To all of these charges the only reply which I can make is that it has worked for me and I hope sincerely it will work for others who are willing to try to tame their tensions.

In conclusion it must be stated that in no way do I lay claim to have discovered all the principles laid out in the pages that follow. They have been gleaned and gathered from dozens of different sources and different people. Perhaps the manner in which they have been applied to my own life is unique. Certainly, to my knowledge this is the first time such ideas have been combined in a single volume which, it is hoped, will help many others.

PART ONE

Physical Life

1

The Body

I begin with the body, not because it is the most important nor because it is of the least consequence, but because it is probably the most obvious area of tension.

From the time a child takes its first faltering steps, accompanied by the fear of falling, to the final twilight years of old age with their anxiety and failing strength, the body is subject to tension.

The small boy who is always concerned about whether he is big enough or tall enough or strong enough to compete with his companions shows stress centered in concern about his body. The teen-age girl who spends agonizing hours of self-appraisal before her mirror reflects the same anxiety about her physical appearance. "Am I pretty enough?" she wonders. "Why did I have to be born with this funny nose and crooked teeth?"

The dreadful dismay over skin blemishes, an inferior figure, or straight hair is enough to give some adolescents a lifetime complex, a complex of feeling under constant scrutiny, constant derision by more favored folk.

I recall clearly the inner foreboding with which I used to face gym classes as a teen-ager. Through no fault of mine, but simply because of lack of milk as a youngster, I had suffered from rickets. The disease left my bones a bit deformed and my body less well shaped than it might have been. To have it exposed to the scrutiny of my classmates and even the gym teacher made me cringe inside. The cutting taunts about knock-knees and narrow shoulders left deep wounds that it took years to erase.

Fortunately those same caustic comments were to act as sharp spurs that drove me to do something about it. I shall refer to that later. But the fact remains that our bodies can be the center of cruel pressures upon our personalities.

And these pressures continue all through life, for in our Western society there is a powerful phobia attached to the illusion that somehow one must remain eternally young. Women in middle age and even in advancing years struggle to maintain their teen-age beauty. Advertising agencies and the mass media lead people to believe that through the use of cosmetics, elaborate wearing apparel, or other physical aids it is possible to retain or regain eternal youth.

It is true, happily, that for a favored few this is possible. Here and there one encounters individuals who appear wonderfully young, attractive, and unmarked by the passing years. But for the great majority of men and women time takes its toll. Their hair turns gray; their teeth decay; their eyes become dim; their hearing fails; their vigor diminishes; their strength slips away; lines and wrinkles crease the skin; memory fades and the body bends beneath the pressure of passing years.

And so because of all this—be it loss of strength, fading beauty, or lack of vitality with impaired health—anxiety, concern, and stress threaten the body's welfare.

Many of us may not realize just how much real tension, anxiety, worry, and concern are thus centered in our bodies. Of course much of the tension is passed indirectly to such things as the clothing we wear, the medicines we take, or even the food we eat. Yet it is the body itself which is under pressure and demands the attention given to it in so many areas of life. These will be dealt with in detail in subsequent chapters. At this point I wish to pause and appraise our general attitude to the body itself as a living organism.

Many of our tensions over our bodies can be relieved by a more sensible and realistic attitude toward them. There are quite literally thousands of men and women who hold a peculiar if not definitely perverted view of the human body.

First of all there are those who somehow feel a sense of shame and guilt that they even own a body. The fundamental fact that it functions by imbibing food and discharging wastes appears to be almost abhorrent. That the body should produce such things as perspiration, urine, loose hair, discarded skin cells, peculiar odors, and feces leaves some people rather disquieted. They seem unable to accept these processes of body metabolism as either natural or normal. Rather the attitude taken is one of trying to cover up and conceal, or at least excuse oneself for normal bodily functions. In all of this there are bound to be anxiety, tension, and a self-conscious fear of "offending" others.

This need not be. The normal, proper, wholesome, relaxed attitude to the body is one in which we simply recognize that it is an intricately complicated organism designed to do exactly what it does. We need offer no excuses nor apologies for its functions. We accept it as it is and marvel at its performance.

Unfortunately, human beings have tended always to pervert everything on the planet. There are those individuals who take peculiar pleasure in degrading anything of merit, value, or beauty. And the human body has come in for more than its share of abuse from those who decry its dignity and deprecate its design. They would have us believe there is something sordid and evil and shameful about its perfectly natural functions and behavior. Under this sense of shame, of "self-excusing," some people suffer all their lives.

All of this is very false and unnecessary. It puts people under a tension to which they need never be subject. The only alternative is a wholesome, happy attitude of self-acceptance

. . . a willingness to accept one's body as it has been built and designed. We need make no apologies whatever for performing what is a perfectly natural function. What is more, it is incredible to realize how efficient are these bodily activities which can in some cases continue for nearly a century without breakdown, given half a chance.

The sooner we acquire a sane and sensible view of the body as something uniquely wondrous in design, the sooner we will tame our tensions over our private toilet.

Much the same attitude is required when it comes to considering the build and configuration of the body. So much has been made both in art and literature of a certain type of physique that those who do not conform to the classic idea of bodily beauty feel frustrated and inferior.

In the Western world the peculiar notion has become popular that to be truly attractive a woman should have 34-24-34 measurements or their equivalents. For men the standards are likewise almost as absurd—dark-haired, six feet tall, broad-shouldered, and narrow-hipped.

For those of us who have traveled to foreign countries and lived among people of other cultures, the absurdity of the above becomes immediately apparent. What constitutes beauty and desirability for a Masai on the plains of East Africa (and they are a magnificent race) is far different from what constitutes beauty for the Japanese or the English. Beauty is essentially in the eye of the beholder. It is not inherently in the structure of a skeleton nor the distribution of flesh upon our framework of bone.

Despite this fundamental fact, human beings go through their entire life tantalized and tortured by the suspicion that they are not beautiful, handsome, or attractive. To such I say simply, "Accept yourself as you are!" This is the first step to quelling the anxiety arising over your bodily appearance. You were born this way; it is not your fault that your body was fashioned to its own peculiar form and figure.

But one need not stop here. There are too many who do! Given a reasonably healthy body with no matter how awkward a figure, it is unbelievable what determination and a bit of self-discipline can do to enhance it. Hints and ideas along this line will be given in subsequent chapters. Suffice it to say at this point that with perseverance and patience it is fantastic what can be done to acquire "the body beautiful."

However, we have the key to at least half of the secret if we honestly believe the body is, in itself, "beautiful." If we feel it is something to be ashamed of, something to be clothed and covered from view, something to be so swathed in cottons, silks, nylon, and wool that it cannot be seen, we are doomed to disappointment in our desire to be relaxed and beautiful.

So much of the tension, stress, and anxiety of our modern society is attached to the idea of being well dressed. Too often we attach undue importance to the art of covering up our defects and deluding the onlooker. The man or woman who possesses a normal, healthy body has nothing to hide. One need not be unduly proud of one's physique. Rather it is a case of knowing calmly and assuredly that your body is fit and vigorous. Because of this it is essentially a beautiful body—not a beauty contest body, but a wholesome, beautiful body. At that point one can relax. Gone are the tension, the anxiety, the worry that someone might discover what a sham you are.

What follows should all help to this one end. It should change you into a more beautiful person both in body, mind, and spirit.

For the sake of young people, especially, it may be useful to point out here that dress in itself does not truly denote the character of the wearer. It may in part express the individual's personality. The extrovert will declare himself with flashy attire while the more modest introvert will be content with conservative clothes. But clothing per se is not the final criterion either of character or of physical fitness.

The fact that someone has good taste in clothing or perchance owns a larger purse with which to purchase more expensive apparel does not indicate any superiority in either body, mind, or spirit. Therefore it follows that clothing fads and fashion as such need not cause the anxiety and tension which they tend to cause with so many. Some of the greatest rogues in the country wear mink coats or pinstripe suits. And just because a few people are willing to be made slaves to the tyranny of fashion does not mean all others should be brought under pressure to comply with the current dictates of how the body should be covered.

Clothing the body should not become the main preoccupation in life, as it does for many. Essential as clothes may be for bodily comfort and protection in inclement weather, they need not become the obsession they tend to become. Instead, as long as they are clean, comfortable, and a pleasure to wear, they have served their basic purpose.

Taken with this attitude the stress and strain of how to dress is diminished and we are at liberty to live in a freer dimension.

The same principle applies to the entire question of personal hygiene and cleanliness. An enormous amount of propaganda and advertising pressure has been brought to bear on the general public about bodily care. The average person believes he or she has no chance of success in life without the unrelenting use of cosmetics, soaps, deodorants, perfumes, and a dozen other bodily emollients.

One need only stroll up and down the aisles of a modern drugstore or chemist's shop to be overwhelmed by the array of preparations for the body. The items run into the thousands and range from toenail polish to false eyelashes, from expensive perfumes to ordinary hand soap. Amid all this the average person is brought under tension, wondering if he or she is keeping up with the times in being handsome or glamorous.

The rather startling truth of the matter is that many of the commodities contribute nothing whatever to one's well-being. They are, rather, an unnecessary expenditure. The benefits, if any, derived from the average purchase are so fleeting and temporary as to hardly warrant the expense. Still, millions of dollars are expended annually on products which it is hoped will help to beautify the body.

The anxiety and strain of struggling to keep up in the area

of beauty aids often undo whatever slight benefit they might bestow. Despite all her cosmetics, the average fashionable woman today shows more stress in her face than does her less sophisticated counterpart who perhaps only splashes cold water on her cheeks to freshen them in the morning.

Even the matter of bathing and showering has become almost a religious rite with millions. Yet it has been demonstrated beyond doubt by medical authorities that the human body naturally covers itself with a protective coating to combat invading organisms. Excessive washing, especially with hot water and soap, removes this protective layer, leaving one more susceptible to disease. Proof of this can be found in remote races of people who seldom bathe yet enjoy an unusually high degree of health.

Such direct benefits to the body as moderate sun bathing are often completely undone by bathing or showering immediately after exposure to sunlight. At least three hours should elapse before washing the skin after exposure to direct sunlight if maximum health is desired.

All of this leads to the very important subject of general bodily health. Few of us pause to think about the marvelous design and functions of the human body; its capacity to cope with wounds, sores, cuts, abrasions, and breakage is almost beyond belief. Too many of us believe that healing lies in the hands of doctors, that remedies can come only out of a bottle, that the prescription for health lies in pills and pharmaceutical products. Nothing could be more absurd. How the medical profession is able to cast its ancient spell of magic on the human mind is of interest. For, were it not for the amazing ability of the body to mend itself (given half a chance), the doctors with all their diagnoses and drugs would be well-nigh powerless to cure diseases or forestall death.

When there dawns upon us an acute awareness of our own inherent ability to mend ourselves, we are halfway to good health. This is not merely a case of mind over matter. It is not self-hypnotism. Rather it is holding a sane, simple, but unshakable confidence in our own capacity to overcome the diseases and disasters which are part and parcel of living.

Of course this is conditional upon our using good sense in our everyday lives. It implies that we will not abuse our bodies. It assumes that the simple steps outlined throughout this book will become the normal and accepted pattern of living. Then our bodies will be given every possible chance to function free of undue stress and strain, able to meet all the demands made upon them.

Whether we wish to admit it or not, literally millions of human beings live under the tension of the fear of ill health. They dread sickness. They fear disease with an overwhelming apprehension. They are terrified at the thought of failing vigor, to say nothing of the dark, anxious dread of death. They are alarmed by every little pain or ache, rushing off to find immediate relief either from a doctor's office or a drugstore counter.

But when the realization comes gently and assuringly to us that we are so designed as to cope with most diseases, a calmness and quietness settle over us. Gone is much of the tension and anxiety attached to our malady. For strange as it may seem, disease flourishes in the atmosphere of fear. Bodies break down more readily under tension. Anxiety actually augments and intensifies any attack made on the body.

My childhood is probably best remembered for the amount of time I spent in bed. Until I was eighteen years of age I scarcely knew what good health was. Tropical dysentery, rickets, malaria, and other diseases had so ravaged my body that I felt only a half-grown boy. My early manhood was marked with incessant abdominal pains which it was said could be relieved only by massive surgery. In my midthirties, I submitted to a major medical examination. The report was that I had only six months left to live so I should make the most of them.

It was then, in the quiet tent camps which I occupied alone in the African bush, that there began to dawn on me that it was tension, anxiety, worry, and stress which were in fact destroying me. It was there under the spreading acacia trees in the foothills of Mount Kilimanjaro, and later on the sands of a quiet Canadian beach that I began to believe my body could beat the damage done to it. And it did. The past twenty-five years have seen me become a fit, energetic man. No doctor or medication has had a part in this restoration— only the practical ideas contained in these pages.

For these reasons I repeat that illness and poor health flourish in the atmosphere of tension and anxiety. But a sublime and sure confidence that our bodies have been built to overcome the assaults made upon them can remove much of the strain and stress, setting us free to function normally and uninhibited by false imaginations.

Along with this awareness that our bodies can combat illness on their own, it is also important to know that they are in fact always changing. It has been shown that approximately every seven years all the cells in the body are replaced with new ones. This means simply that we are being constantly remade and renewed. Naturally this in no way guarantees perpetual life, for ultimately the passing of time demands that death must come. After all, absolutely nothing on earth, even the planet itself, is guaranteed eternal duration. Only the spirit of man, which I shall deal with later, is given this great honor.

But this continuous renewal of the body should give us great hope and great good cheer to believe that things are very much better than we might think or feel. And again it enables us to tame the tension which arises when we might otherwise feel our time is up. In other words, in the knowledge of this incredible self-renewal, proceeding without any particular awareness on my part, I am able to relax and enjoy living in a deep dimension.

Finally, in a discussion of this sort it is most important to point out the patterns of normal monthly behavior to which the body is subject. It is surprising to discover just how few people are aware they they live under the constant ebb and flow of definite physiological cycles that condition and control their bodies.

Of course it is common knowledge that women have to contend with their menstrual cycles. The increasing tension as menstruation approaches is so real and so demanding in some cases that it poses a crisis period each month. In the case of married couples, unless both man and wife are acutely aware of this condition and its attendant pressures, it can be a most difficult time. Then more than at any other period in the month extra tenderness, thoughtfulness, and consideration are needed to alleviate stress in the home. More marriage breakups begin at this point than any other, simply because under pressure the woman may act in an aggravated manner which annoys and alienates her husband.

Over and above the very obvious menstrual cycle in women there is a corresponding though much less conspicuous biological cycle in men. Most of them would be reluctant to admit it, but still it exists and has a direct bearing on their behavior. It explains why on some days a man may behave like a bear for no good reason whatever. Most men cannot really understand themselves or fathom why they can be so mean.

In addition to these purely biological cycles in both men and women there are two other cycles of rising and falling intensity. One is purely physical—a fluctuation in energy output which covers a period of approximately thirty to thirty-five days. In full flood it leaves the individual feeling zestful, fit, and energetic as though he were on top of the world. At its ebb the person is inclined to be "down," lacking initiative and strength, and wondering why. So critical is this cycle that some of the greatest athletes keep careful charts to determine the dates when maximum output of energy will be available.

Then there is a physiological cycle which has emotional as well as physical implications. It too has an enormous influence on how one "feels." It will be seen that if perchance two or more of these cycles should coincide at the same time, for they are not necessarily of the same duration, a person can be subjected to enormous depression (oppression) or, conversely, carried to great heights of exalted elation.

The rise and fall of changing feelings exerts terrible tension on some people. The important point is simply to recognize and accept the fact that one's body does fluctuate in the way it feels. In this knowledge fear and foreboding vanish and one learns to live with oneself. A point of particular help and interest to remember is this: whenever you feel most weak and downcast, take heart. Actually, the lowest point has already been passed and one's body has already begun a new buildup of energy.

Tomorrow is bound to be better than today. What seems so impossible now will appear ever so much more feasible then. All is not dark! There is a silver lining to the engulfing cloud. Just knowing this to be the case removes the worry and eases the terrible tension that tends to grip us.

Last, but by no means least important, are tensions produced in the body by changing weather conditions. In former times, when a greater proportion of our people lived in rural areas, there was a keener awareness of atmospheric changes and their influence on human beings than now. Urban life with its indoor mode of living tends to make us less conscious of weather.

In spite of this, the passage of high and low pressure ridges and the approach of cyclone and anticyclone weather systems have a profound effect on some people. Likewise, some animals are very sensitive to barometric changes. As the pressure increases, there is a noticeable increase in tenseness, nervousness, irritability, and moroseness.

For several years my family and I lived on a part of British Columbia's west coast where all winter long we were exposed to a continuous progression of intermittent high and low pressure systems. It scarcely affected my wife, but worked havoc with my well-being. Not until we had moved away to an area with a more stable climate did I comprehend the relentless pressures that had put me under terrible tension for months at a time.

Accordingly I recommend very earnestly that individuals should first of all find out if they are sensitive to atmospheric pressures. If they are, then, in their own best interests they should live where local climate conditions do not fluctuate frequently or affect them adversely.

It is worthy of mention that in recent years detailed studies have been made of alcoholism in the various sections of North America. A surprising conclusion was that areas subjected to intense and continuous barometric changes have the highest rate of alcoholism. The deep-rooted desire to "escape" the repeated changes finds release in drink. But this is only to bring oneself under a new and even more ruthless form of oppression. The sane and sensible alternative is to find an area with a more stable climate where the effects of changing weather patterns are less detrimental.

From the various views about bodily pressures expressed in this chapter, it is sincerely hoped direct and lasting benefit will be brought to the reader. At first some of the thoughts may seem too simple, too ordinary, even too obvious. Yet it is amazing how few people act on them in earnestness. Those who do will discover that they have emerged into a new and vibrant dimension of deeper understanding. They will have learned to handle pressures on themselves. To a degree they will have begun to tame those tensions which in the past oppressed them like tyrants.

In the chapters which follow, some practical and detailed hints are given on how to treat our bodies, how to care for these amazing organisms with which we have been endowed so that they will flourish happily.

A calm, cheerful acceptance of our bodies is made more feasible if we appreciate that they are the masterpieces of a complex creation. Only the wisdom, skill, and ingenuity of God, our Father, could ever fashion an organism of such astonishing and wondrous capabilities. They can be to us a symbol of the sublime intellect and marvelous mind of our loving Father. Because of this we should treat them with the dignity, care, and respect they deserve.

2

Outdoor Living

The human body was not intended for indoor living. It was not designed to function at its best within the confines of a city. Stale air, smog, polluted water, excessive noise, cramped quarters, lack of sunshine, and little exercise are all hard on the body. They put it under pressures and strains which it finds difficult to deal with adequately.

This may seem to be a series of startling statements. Certainly they may come as a distinct shock to those who have grown up and lived in cities all their lives, accepting the urban environment as a perfectly normal way of life.

That millions of men and women do spend their lives in such places and manage to make it from the cradle to the grave in a stumbling sort of fashion does not in any way deny the truth of what has been said. It does demonstrate, however, how adaptable and rugged the human body can be, enduring such abuse for so long and still surviving reasonably well.

From youth I held a peculiar and powerful aversion to cities and all that they represented. An overwhelming revulsion would engulf me every time I had to go into a city or spend time living in one. A tremendous, almost terrifying sense of tension and pressure would descend upon me, making me yearn to escape to the clean air and open sunshine of the countryside.

People would ridicule me for this. They literally laughed at my dislike of the modern metropolis. Sometimes I was suspiciously regarded almost as somewhat of a grouch and eccentric when it came to the subject of cities and their impact on people.

Detailed studies and extensive research into human behavior have gradually brought to light ample proof of the formidable, adverse forces in the city which I had so long feared. It is now commonly recognized and agreed that the manmade environments of our urban communities are really atrocious places for people to spend their lives in.

Newspapers, books, magazines, radio broadcasts, and TV programs are packed with reports of pollution and the destruction of our environment. It is probably the most popular theme in the world today. Everybody talks about it; most people show some concern; only a few attempt to correct the situation or improve their own particular part in the picture.

This chapter is an honest attempt to share some of the simple ideas which I have found practical in everyday living even under city conditions. After all, most of the world's people now live in cities; so realistic advice must be available on how to handle the pressures placed upon individuals in that sort of atmosphere.

Perhaps the most important factor that will help counteract the tension of city life is to enjoy as much outdoor living as possible. This is not easy to do, especially in the very large metropolitan areas where the nearest open country may be miles away. Still there are always fragments of open space and open skies in city parks, greenbelts, and even small secluded gardens, sundecks, or rooftops. Wherever they are, these should be sought out deliberately and diligently. For it is there one can, at least for a few moments in the day, be set free from the stress and strain of his usual surroundings.

During one period of my early manhood I was sent by the government to serve for six months in a gigantic factory where thousands of employees were crowded together building aircraft. Not only were my immediate surroundings almost intolerable, but to compound the horror of the place it was located in a low-lying, swampy area where fog was common. Consequently, opportunities for finding fresh air, sunshine, or natural beauty to offset the steel and concrete walls of my world were very slim. I recall, clearly, however, my delight in discovering behind one of the huge hangars a few square yards of green grass that had escaped the bulldozers. It ran down to the murky river nearby; on the opposite bank a fringe of trees survived. Best of all, the grassy spot was a sun trap where one could go at noon and coffee breaks to escape the factory fumes and never-ending noise.

Those few yards of open ground, clothed in green grass, open to the sky, and overlooking the river, saved my sanity in that manmade inferno. More than that, they preserved my body from breaking down beneath the appalling pressures on me. My chum and I would slip out to our "sanctuary" at every opportunity. There we would soak up a little sunshine, breathe deeply of the open air, walk briskly on the soft sod, and fill our vision with the quiet views across the river.

Sunshine, fresh air, and moderate exercise can do more to relieve the strain of modern living than can anything else. Best of all, these are all for free, requiring no cost but the bare time required to take them. Of course there are those who will argue that time is very precious, that they haven't got any to spare, that if they did it would not be wasted on such trifles as sunshine, fresh air, or exercise.

My reply to these people is that if they prefer to break down under the tension of twentieth-century living, to have their cases carefully diagnosed by a well-paid physician, and finally to try to find their feet again by spending a spell in a hospital ward or at home in bed, that is entirely their business.

But to the rest I appeal in all simplicity to seek the sun, the open skies, some fresh air, and some physical exercise at every opportunity. At the very least, this is excellent health insurance. At best, it is a road which can very well lead to a life of new zest, eager vitality, reduced tension, and a relaxed frame of mind.

First of all let us think about sunshine . . . just plain ordinary sunlight. Perhaps it is not quite as common as it may seem. For one thing, with increasing smog, high-rise buildings, greater atmospheric pollution, and more indoor occupations people have less chance than ever of seeing the sun. Maybe this explains in part the mania for acquiring a tan. Human beings swing from one extreme to the other. So in cities where they have few opportunities to become bronzed they still want others to believe they are the bold, rugged, outdoor type.

Apart from all this, one should seek the sun, at least for a few moments each day. If it is possible to disrobe, even in part, and expose a greater portion of the body to its beneficial effect, this should be done. A little thought and planning can frequently find some secluded spot where one can relax under the sun's warm rays for a short spell.

Exposure in this way has three immediate positive benefits. The first is that just being outdoors in the sunshine brightens one's outlook on all of life for the day. For, "as long as the sun shines, things can't be too black or dark." Sometimes after a troubled or restless night in which sleep has been absent and the mind and body tossed feverishly, what a benediction to see the sun break over the horizon and brighten all the world!

This going out into the sun lifts the load on life. It takes us out of the close confines of our cramped living quarters. It reassures us that all is not wrong. It lifts the heart and relaxes the mind. It eases the strain and tension of living.

Secondly, exposing ourselves to sunlight, especially if we can do it stretched out full length, is an amazing therapeutic treatment. With the body freed of constricting clothing, bared to the gentle caress and warm touch of sunlight, one can relax with utter serenity. No other single habit has provided me with greater relief from the tensions which would otherwise tyrannize me.

There is a need in all of this to leave our worries behind, to allow the mind to rest quietly, and, if it so happens, even to drift off in gentle slumber for a few moments.

Evidence that this is a universally beneficial habit can be seen in animal behavior. All forms of life from enormous elephants down to the smallest birds and mammals revel in the relaxation afforded by stretching out in the sun. It is of the essence of harmony with one's surroundings, and in its own wondrous way makes us sure the whole world is not awry.

The third benefit of enjoying the sun is its physical effect on the body. It is the best possible means of absorbing vitamin D. This vitamin in combination with calcium in the body insures healthy nerves and a quiet, calm, contented outlook. Without adequate amounts of vitamin D, calcium cannot be properly assimilated by the body. I like to call calcium the "calmer" because of its help in easing tension. So, ample sunshine combined with plenty of calcium can help us to be much less susceptible to strain or stress.

Indirectly, too, the tanning effect of sunshine helps to boost our morale. Somehow we sense and know we look more fit, and this in itself is a tonic to us.

It is a debatable point whether or not exposure to sunlight can alleviate arthritis. However, the deep penetration of the sun's rays, together with its therapeutic value, may accomplish much. It has been said arthritis is aggravated by worry and anxiety. If so, then the relief of strain by sunbathing is bound to benefit the sufferer. At one point I was so crippled by arthritis in my back and hips that at times I could not get off a couch. Since exposing myself regularly to sunlight this malady has almost entirely disappeared and I am now virtually free of it.

Next to sunshine, perhaps the most important ingredient in the outdoors for our well-being is fresh air. Of course in some of our large cities it is well-nigh impossible to find unpolluted air. It horrified me to be told that in the center of New York City the streets' ornamental trees and flowering shrubs had to be replaced each spring because at best they could survive only a single season. If this be true of trees, imagine the damage done to human beings who must live under the influence of such contaminated air.

Nevertheless there must be some sort of effort made in this direction if one is to enjoy even a modest degree of vigorous health. Often less-polluted air can be found in the vicinity of open parks, lake shores, the seaside, riverbanks, and any undeveloped areas where trees, brush, or vegetation grows. Even the plants and shrubs in a modest garden help to purify the air. One should seek such spots and there inhale deeply of the atmosphere. Most of us use only a fraction of our lung capacity. We literally starve our bodies of oxygen and function like faltering engines.

In our quest for fresh air and sunshine, it is possible to combine two very beneficial bodily exercises at once. These are deep breathing and walking.

The desirability of drawing great drafts of fresh, clean air into the lungs cannot be overstated. Not only does the fresh air provide the lungs, liver, and circulatory system with generous supplies of oxygen, but it also produces a powerful surge of new vigor and vitality to the entire body. Often when we are in a great forest, beside the sea, or at the edge of open fields, we should pause purposely to inhale deeply of the delicious fresh air wafted to us on the wind. There sweeps over one an almost intoxicating charge of supreme well-being. As the fresh flow of oxygen surges through the bloodstream, one can sense its cleansing force flushing away the old stale wastes that have accumulated. As the deep breathing continues, strength, vigor, and vitality permeate every part of the body, making one feel totally alive and energetic.

Most of us don't know how to breathe deeply regularly. It has been said that most people use only about 30 percent of their total lung capacity. Actually there is a general habit of using only the top section of our lungs; this is of itself insufficient to charge the body with an optimum supply of oxygen.

If, on the other hand, one deliberately sets out to breathe deeply, consciously driving air into the very bottom of the lungs, an enormous difference can be felt in general fitness.

For example, regular deep breathing is one of the finest beauty aids there is. It far surpasses facial massage or the use of cosmetics. The surge of oxygen-charged blood to the surface of the skin not only gives it a beautiful glow and color but activates all the skin cells, making one appear totally alive and alert.

Those who consciously concentrate on deep breathing and the proper use of the diaphragm soon find their entire physique improving. It is literally impossible to breathe deeply without standing erect and holding one's body in a stately position. No other habit will so quickly correct poor posture and give one the bearing of a king or queen.

I have a cousin who was my mother's favorite niece. As a young girl it was soon apparent that she would mature into a very tall woman. Instead of regarding this as a disadvantage, she was fortunate to find a friend who encouraged her to stand as straight and erect as possible. "If you are going to be tall, Beth, you might just as well be beautiful." She learned to stand and walk erect by regular deep breathing. She bore herself with a regal beauty. Her posture was so superb people paused to admire her. Added to this was the double benefit of possessing a beautiful face and glowing complexion. Anyone going through life this way is bound to feel much more buoyant, much more alive, much less depressed or under tension than the one who drags around half-alive.

Now deep-breathing exercises, in themselves, can be a bit of a bore. This does not mean that they cannot be done, but they should be combined with some other congenial exercise.

It is at this point that I emphasize the double benefit of combining deep breathing with walking. Some more energetic people may prefer to run, or jog. This is excellent provided it does not become somewhat of a penance. I recall meeting a very aged gentleman running on the beach one day in intense heat. I felt compelled to speak to him, warning of the dangers of overexertion at his age and under such adverse conditions. He replied that he was determined to become "as fit as any young fellow," which may be a fine ideal but scarcely an ambition a man in his seventies is likely to attain.

It is appropriate to point out here the futility of older people attempting to remain eternally young. It is neither normal nor natural to expect this. To do so is simply to put ourselves under undue stress by trying to attain the impossible. As the years roll by we can remain fit, well, and vigorous. We can be buoyant in spirit and cheerful in outlook. But we cannot be forever young. Once one accepts this fact much of the frustration of failing strength vanishes and we learn to live content with the energy we possess.

There are, of course, exceptions to every rule. I knew an aged gentleman well into his eighties who lived in a small, unpretentious cabin on the cold Canadian prairies. So strong, so vigorous, and so resilient was his body that at the age of eighty-four he would still work all day, shoveling coal by hand onto his truck and then unloading it into customers' basements. Much of this heavy manual labor he performed in winter weather when the mercury was well below zero. But for every man of this sort there are a multitude of those who must learn to live gently in their declining years.

No matter what a man's or woman's age may be, however, deep breathing while out walking can be the elixir of life. As a people we in the West have long since lost the art of walking. Automobiles and other mechanical conveyances have robbed us of this joy. A daily walk can indeed be the highlight of the day's physical activites.

There is much more to walking than merely getting from one place to another. In fact it should not ever be allowed to become a boring routine. If it does, then half of its benefits are lost. Rather it should be an interlude in the day's activities to which we look forward and which we relish with deep delight. A certain keen expectation and eagerness to get outdoors into the fresh air and sunshine should characterize a walk. It needs to be something we really want to do.

Once one is outdoors, dressed appropriately for the prevailing weather, one can leave the cares and pressures of the workaday world. This is absolutely essential. It is pointless to walk and worry. To do this is simply to amplify the fret one feels, for with every footstep the gnawing anxiety and apprehension will simply be blown up and accentuated.

When one sets out for a walk, there should be as deliberate an attempt to fling open the windows of one's soul and mind to new views as there is to open wide the body to inhale fresh air. A feeling of adventure and new expectation should grip us, shaking away the clinging cobwebs of accumulated worries and tensions of the past twenty-four hours.

This is not easy to do, especially if one has not tried it before. At first, despite one's best efforts, the old anxieties keep creeping back into the subconscious and there reexerting their pressure. But one must persevere, and with time this will become one of the beautiful interludes of the day in which both mind and body as well as spirit are set free from the tyranny of our tensions.

It is the actual physical activity of walking itself which is such a help here. One should not just slouch or saunter along casually. Rather a brisk, vigorous, comfortable pace should be set. The body should be held erect with head up, chest out, and arms swinging freely.

Deliberately and determinedly breathe deeply, not just as an exercise, but rather as though one were drinking deeply of a delicious drink. In fact that is precisely what one is doing, drinking deeply—inhaling deeply—of the delicious fresh air outdoors. As one does this a keen sense of physical and mental exhilaration will be experienced. Gradually an increasing awareness of one's surroundings engulfs the walker. The mind is quickened; the senses are alerted; the whole being is intensely alive.

In this state of heightened awareness, one is better able to open up to all the impressions coming in from the world around. Perhaps it is the pattern of passing cloud shadows on the ground. Perchance it is the plaintive call of a wild bird from a nearby bush. Maybe it is the gentle touch of wind on the cheek or raindrops on the face. It could be the fragrance of damp earth or the perfume of a plant in flower. It is sometimes just the fleeting smile from a stranger passing by on the path.

Whatever the sensation be, cherish it deeply. Be glad you

can see, smell, hear, feel, or touch it with your entire being. This puts a man or woman, though walking alone, in close touch with the earth, with the universe, with the essence of all life that shares the planet with us. And beyond this it puts us in touch with the sublime, the divine, the goodness of God our heavenly Father.

There is something tremendously uplifting, very strengthening, very energizing to be reminded again that we are a part of His care and His concern. There comes again the reassurance that life is not all evil, that whatever the pressures upon us may be, there are other counterforces at work just as energetically on our behalf, directed by God Himself.

So as we walk vigorously in the open, we find ourselves reinvigorated in body, recharged in mind, and refreshed in spirit. Coming in after such an interlude in the fresh air and sunshine, we are better fitted to cope with the complexities and pressures which are so much a part of modern life.

There are bound to be those for whom the sort of exercise just described will not be sufficiently strenuous. They will want to tire themselves a little more, if for no other reason than to reduce weight or sleep better at night.

This attitude can be readily appreciated. In my own case I have combined running with walking. I am more energetic than some people and find that a few strenuous spurts of running intermingled with walking do wonders for me. When the weather is warm, I enjoy a vigorous swim in the sea. In all of this there is real merit. I still love to tackle a mountain, and a day's hard physical work in a garden is still a joy. Even several sets of tennis are a tonic once in a while. None of these activities are to be deprecated. The only thing to be borne in mind is that moderation in all of them is a wise practice.

There is great good to be had from hobbies which take one outdoors. Even such arts as skating and ballet can be practiced in the open air where their benefit will be twice as great. Men and women who take up gardening, bird watching, rock hounding, driftwood gathering, or nature studies of any sort are on a path that will relieve them of many pressures.

In brief I would put it this way. Nature in all her moods has the magic ability to mend and heal the hurts of life. In her own winsome way she can tame many of the tensions we endure if we but give her the chance by getting outdoors.

3

Rest

It is natural to expect that anyone who follows the suggestions outlined in the previous chapters will be sufficiently relaxed to find that rest comes easily. Oddly enough, this is not always the case.

Many of us are so victimized by worry and anxiety that sleep, especially, eludes us, and just to relax becomes one of the hardest things to do. To all of this the simplest antidote is plain physical tiredness. The man or woman who has experienced the wholesome benefits of bodily exertion, abundant fresh air, and ample sunshine is bound to sleep.

The duration of sleep varies with each person. Some have ample sleep with seven hours. Others may require eight, nine, or even ten hours each night to feel fully refreshed. There are those who feel sleepy by nine o'clock at night and are ready to retire then. Others stay up until well past midnight, doing their best work while others sleep. These are all personal peculiarities to which one must adjust one's individual life and pattern of social behavior. It might be pointed out that in the case of married couples real difficulties can arise if their sleeping patterns are very different. Certain generous attitudes must be cultivated between marriage partners if one enjoys sleeping at the time the other wishes to be awake and hard at work. It takes a degree of tolerance for a night owl to put up with a sleepyhead who drifts off to dreamland about nine o'clock. It takes no less patience for the early riser who loves to greet the dawn to watch his or her partner sleep away the best part of the day between the sheets.

To reduce tension in this area of living does require a definite understanding of the peculiarities of people. It calls for a clear comprehension that what is normal for me may seem very abnormal for my mate. Once this is achieved, friction can be reduced and sensible solutions can be found.

A note of interest and value which has recently been determined by exhaustive research is that the body can rest and be refreshed if one just lies quietly at night, even though not asleep. For years it was assumed only sound sleep could really rest the body. Consequently anyone who did not or could not sleep became concerned, anxious, and distressed over insomnia. Now it is known that the body can benefit just as much if one lies quietly and relaxed, even though not asleep. In this knowledge alone there is relief and freedom from tension for the person who would otherwise toss and turn feverishly throughout the long night.

For those who feel cheated on their sleep at night I have long recommended a noonday nap or siesta. This has been a secret renewal for some of the world's greatest men and women. Leaders like Sir Winston Churchill who were under great stress and strain for months at a stretch found "forty winks" during the day reduced tension and fortified the body as nothing else could. To be able to take these quick catnaps requires the ability to relax, which is an art some people never master.

I am here passing along several suggestions for falling asleep which have been shared with me. Each has its own merit and almost all will work if practiced patiently and persistently.

First of all, one must really want to sleep! This seems

strange to say. It is surprising how many people go to bed just to woolgather, worry, or allow their minds to wander all over the world. But if we are to sleep we must want to sleep and apply our powers of concentration to it. So if one is preoccupied with falling asleep one cannot also be occupied with other worries or anxieties.

Having made up one's mind to sleep, several simple methods can be followed. Probably the easiest and most effective is to see or think black and black alone. By this is not meant to be despondent or downcast. It is the mental discipline of setting oneself to see only the color (or, more accurately, total absence of color) black. The moment any other color, idea, shape, thought, or form intrudes itself, it should be dismissed. Concentrate only on black and in a surprisingly few moments you will be off to sleep.

The second most effective method to ease tension and relax the body is deep, even breathing. Simply stretch out comfortably so that the body is limp. Start to inhale deeply, evenly, and deliberately from the diaphragm as one does when asleep. Try to get up to twenty even breaths, then on the twenty-first hold the breath as long as possible, and repeat. It will be found after trying this a few times that not more than a dozen even breaths are required to completely relax the body and bring on sweet sleep.

The third method, which is probably the most difficult to master, is one of gradual relaxation. Strange to say it has proved the most effective in cases of confirmed, lifelong victims of insomnia.

Again one begins by lying in a relaxed, limp, comfortable position, preferably flat on the back. The arms and legs should be stretched out and relaxed, the head slightly supported by a small soft pillow.

Now one starts to concentrate on relaxing the entire body, not all at once, but by degrees, beginning with the very top of the head, working gradually down toward the toes. Start with the scalp; make sure that it is not tight or taut. Now the forehead—no furrows or wrinkles or tension across your brain. Down to the eyes; let them close and the lids feel heavy. Follow across the face. Allow the cheeks to sag softly. The jaws should not be set nor the teeth clenched. Now to the neck and throat. Relax the large muscles supporting your head. Feel it weighing heavily on the pillow like a limp load.

And so one proceeds on down—the shoulders, chest, the arms, the abdomen, hips, and finally the legs.

Anyone doing this conscientiously will be utterly amazed how difficult it is to do at first. Before he reaches his throat his scalp may be tense again. Yet with practice it is surprising how readily one can learn to "just let go." With experience at the game one generally gets no further than the face before he is asleep.

A fourth method is probably the least well known, but especially helps those of us who love to lie or bask in the sun. It requires less concentration than the others and more imagination.

Simply stretch out on the bed in your favorite position for suntanning on the beach. Picture yourself on some beautiful, warm sandy coastline in summer. Imagine the gentle lap of the waves on the shore. You sense again the gentle caress of warm sunshine on your body. Embraced by these beautiful, relaxing sensations, you find yourself soon asleep.

My first wife, who suffered excruciating pains with cancer before her death, used this method to fall asleep right up to the end of her life. It was more effective than any sedative or sleeping pills ever prescribed for her. She was a person who had always loved the sea. Her beautiful body was tanned to golden glory every summer, and the touch of sun had always been a tremendous tonic to her throughout life. She was not a good sleeper but found this method the best of any for easing her anxieties and falling asleep under tension.

This brings us back to the entire question of sunbathing. The warmth and comfort of sunlight on the skin cannot be overemphasized. And for those fortunate enough to live in sunny climates, there is no better place to take a wee nap each day than in the sun. In very hot climates it is not wise to do this around midday. But before eleven in the morning and after three in the afternoon, there is plenty of time to take a brief rest in the sun. Do not be reluctant to strip down and allow your body the enormous benefit of an hour or so of fresh air and sunshine.

I personally know of no greater panacea for all the pressures and tensions that might play upon us. Often during this brief interlude one drifts off into a deep, relaxed sleep. It is an amazing antidote for anxiety. One awakens fully rested, completely relaxed, and genuinely refreshed. Such sunbaths are recommended to everyone everywhere. These precious interludes should not be filled up with reading the paper, books, magazines, or listening to a radio. They should be special times just for complete and total relaxation.

The whole question of resting and relaxation is not only intensely interesting but also rather complex. There are a good many people who have a decided guilt complex about resting, especially during the day. Deep down inside, there persists the gnawing suspicion that somehow one just shouldn't stop for a bit of a rest. Frequently these are the very people who push themselves to the point where there is a breakdown followed by enforced rest in a hospital.

To help one over this hurdle it is well to remember that the body and brain both function more efficiently if given an occasional break from steady work. Any time lost taking a brief rest is more than made up by increased output of energy after some relaxation.

Over and beyond this there is the basic, indisputable fact that rest is the finest form of health insurance in which one can invest. The person who takes the time to see his or her body and brain are not overworked or overextended will last longest.

The Chinese, with their ancient culture and very great philosophical insights, have coined a phrase which means much—"He who travels gently, travels far." It is a tremendous truth. Not only does it apply in caring for our bodies, but in every other area of human activity and endeavor. The sure path to sudden tragedy and disaster is to rush along relentlessly believing that one's body, soul, and spirit can be abused and driven remorselessly. It cannot be done; the path of life is littered with the wreckage of those who thought they could keep going without letup.

Even being able to relax at night before retiring seems beyond some. They have never learned to turn away from the feverish frenzy of the day's activities. They know nothing of the gentle grace of going to bed free from the fret and cares of life.

There are a few very simple and practical aids to learning this fine art. First one needs to face the fact that the day is done. What has been done simply cannot now be undone. There is no point in punishing oneself with remorse or recrimination over possible wrong decisions or uncompleted tasks. Tomorrow will be another day in which to strive to do better. If there has been any special event or incident of joy, pleasure, and cheerful gaiety, it is good to relive it, being grateful for the good and noble aspects of the day. Thank God for such benefits.

Rather than allowing the last moments of the day to be filled with TV shows that are full of horror, tension, and anxious situations, sit down instead, quietly, with a good book that soothes your conscious mind and leads you to laugh or smile. This is not the time to read books that are so full of tension and excitement that they compel you to carry on, rushing from page to page in breathless expectancy. The book should be one that can be picked up at random, read with relaxation, then laid aside as soon as your eyelids become heavy.

If you are fortunate enough to own an open fireplace, by all means enjoy it briefly before bed. There are certainly not enough open hearths in homes today. But where there is, no greater guarantee of gentle slumber can be found for the soul willing to stretch out before its lovely glow. The flickering flames, the cozy warmth, the sense of genial well-being will bring one swiftly to sweet, deep sleep.

Then there is music. Again, as with books, there is need to be wise and discreet in selecting the sort of music that has a soporific influence on one's personality. Some music can startle us wide awake. Martial music or stirring symphonies can stimulate us to an enormous degree. Instead we should choose the kind of music that personally suits our own mellow moods. It should be music of a sort that soothes us and leaves the impression of quiet contentment. There are few influences which can tame tension as can the right music at the right time.

When our children were growing up we made it a practice in our home to play good music almost every evening about the time they went to bed. As a result, we were spared the tirades and tantrums which are shown by many youngsters at bedtime. In fact sleep came sweetly and swiftly. What is more, as the years went on music became very much a part of our home. The children would often ask me to play some favorite record or sit at the piano and let my fingers ramble over the keys while they drifted off into dreamland.

It might be added here as an aside that children and teenagers are incapable of choosing the books, magazines, and music that are best for them. This is the serious responsibility of the parents. Mother and Dad should make it their concern to introduce their children to fine literature, noble art, and good music. As the youngsters mature, they will develop an appetite for the sort of music, books, and paintings which uplift and ennoble their lives rather than ruin them.

All of this may seem to be for the reader a long way from the subject of rest. It really is not. It is intrinsically bound up with it. Again and again I have gone into homes where within two steps of the door I sensed a terrible tension. There was stress so obvious that it was as if the whole atmosphere were charged with high voltage electrical currents. Mother and Father bristled and were edgy; children screamed and snarled; there were clamor and confusion and chaos.

In part this could perhaps be attributed to personality problems. But more often the reasons were much less difficult to diagnose. From one room the radio might be blaring out some banal songs; on the TV there would be a murder or scandal in full swing; the couch and side tables would be littered with lurid paperbacks or pornographic magazines; and the walls would be decorated with modern mad art.

All of these assorted influences generate tension, stress, and conflict within the close confines of the home. It is not surprising that brother is set against sister, mother against father, or children against parents. The total impact of mad music, lurid literature, and provocative pictures is far beyond what most of us are aware of. We simply cannot be exposed to such influences without a buildup of stress.

The only antidote known for this condition is a total, drastic change in the atmosphere we create in our homes. Not only should there be good music, fine books, and wholesome magazines always available, but even the walls should be adorned with attractive art, handsome paintings, and peaceful scenes.

This does not mean we have to be connoisseurs of the finest in art. It does not imply that we have to become ardent art collectors. But it does involve a definite and deliberate effort to find a few choice pictures which convey peace and tranquility into the setting of our homes.

I recall very vividly the elation which was mine when one day in a small prairie town I came across an exquisite mountain scene in a small furniture shop. The grand price for the print was just over ten dollars. But so serene and so sublime was the composition of that particular picture that scores and scores of visitors who came to call on us would simply stand spellbound before it. It silently but inexorably cast a spell of quiet strength, beauty, and composure over our living room.

It is simple things like this that so often spell the difference between tension and turmoil on the one hand, and quiet restfulness on the other. Even a crude log cabin which was once my retreat, high in the hills of central British Columbia, had its rough walls ornamented with lovely pictures of pastoral scenes. And, again, those who came to call on us there always commented how peaceful the cabin seemed. In part it was simply the happy, cheerful pictures pinned to the log walls which helped to create the atmosphere of tranquility where tensions were tamed.

Bringing an occasional bouquet of flowers into the home helps to soften the scene and cheer the heart. These need not be expensive flower arrangements bought from the florist. Like some other things already mentioned in this book, the best things are often free. Over and over you can bring home nothing more than a few pine twigs taken from a wild tree, perhaps a spray of marsh grass adorned with a cattail, maybe a bit of gnarled root or twisted limb with clinging cones, sometimes only a handful of shining stones or sparkling seashells. Whatever you like, do bring some natural beauty into your home. And as the day draws to a close contemplate the loveliness of what there is at hand. Lose yourself just a little in the fragrance of a flower, the rough symmetry of a cone, the feel of a wave-smoothed shell, the colors of autumn in a leaf, or the glow of lamplight on a bit of stone.

All of these are part and parcel of a long-enduring planet. They are fragments from the fabric of a wondrous universe. They are beyond the petty fret that gnaws at your subconscious. They are a bit of our Father's love for us.

Just focusing one's attention on something tangible in this way relieves the tension which otherwise grips the mind and imagination. If one has a mate or companion, late evening is the ideal time to discuss in leisure the innumerable array of natural interests generated by the objects in view. In contrast the hour before retiring is no time to think about all the problems and complexities of your life. Give yourself a break from this anxiety before bed.

Another practice which is most helpful and conducive to quiet rest at night is a very short little walk outdoors before turning in. It is a great consolation for man and wife to take a gentle stroll together, arm in arm, under the mellow light of moon, stars, and setting sun. It draws them together. It restores that special touch of oneness. It rekindles the glow of gentle warmth and tenderness between two people deeply devoted. It takes a little time and trouble, but it is better than any artificial therapy for quieting minds and contenting hearts. The benefits of some fresh air and a short walk are found in refreshing slumber.

For those of us who are older, experience has shown that we sleep better if our late evening meal is not a heavy one.

Meals with too much meat or other high-protein food as well as stimulating drinks like tea or coffee can detract from sleep and disturb one's dreams.

It would not be right to end this chapter on rest without mentioning a thought or two about beds and bedrooms. After all, roughly a third of one's life is spent in sleep. Where we sleep should be given some careful thought and attention.

The bedroom should be located where there is a minimum of disturbance at night. It should be located as far as possible from the street and major noise-producing areas of the home. It should be well ventilated, yet warm enough for comfortable rest. There should be blinds thick enough to darken the room well without blocking all air. It is generally true to say that the body rests better if conditions are slightly cool rather than too warm. Most of us dread hot summer nights when heat and humidity make rest difficult and the night a torment.

It is not uncommon, for maximum rest, to use comforters or other light, warm bedding rather than too many heavy blankets.

Bulky or heavy nightclothes should be avoided. Too often they tend to entwine the body and restrict freedom of movement in bed. More and more people sleep in very light attire and sleep better because of it. Nor does it do any harm to allow the entire body to enjoy an air bath for a few moments before and after retiring. This is especially desirable if one's occupation demands the wearing of restrictive clothing during the day.

About beds it is probably sufficient to say that a firm, well-built mattress is an excellent investment. Sleeping on it should be not only a benefit to the body but part of the joy of life itself.

4

Eating

The reader may wonder why a chapter in this book on taming tension should be taken up with eating. Surely it would seem that this is an area of life where we can relax and just enjoy our food. If this last statement were true, there would be no need for a chapter on the subject. The facts of life prove, however, beyond doubt, that what we eat, when, and how are all of deep concern to people. So it is proper that a few practical, helpful suggestions be given.

Some have gone so far as to say, "You are what you eat." By this they mean that the type of food we consume in large measure determines the kind of people we are. There is a degree of truth to this, but it is not the entire story.

Books and books have been written and published just on the subject of human nutrition. Likewise all sorts of books and pamphlets have been written on exercise, sports, and physical fitness. As a matter of fact there is scarcely a subject touched on in this book about which dozens of other books have not already been written. But where the chief difficulty lies is in the narrow approach which most authors take to their work. Far too many hold the view that if you just eat correctly, all will be well. Or if you just practice certain calisthenics or exercises, you will be fit. Or if you just hold the proper attitude of mind, life can be beautiful.

In part they are perfectly correct. In part they are equally wrong. Life to be full and complete must have all of its attributes attended to with care, and diet is no exception. Consequently I make no apologies for giving a few pages to the subject of food. It has an enormous influence upon us and deserves our attention.

We have to recognize that the three greatest personal drives or desires in any animal organism are for (1) space, room, or territory in which to survive; (2) food to support life in the allotted space; (3) reproduction to assure the perpetuation of the race.

In primitive societies it was of course taken for granted that if one had sufficient space or territory it automatically insured that he had an adequate supply of food. For example, if one or one's tribe held sway over so much hunting territory, or grazing lands, or garden ground, or fishing waters, he was sure of food for himself and his family provided the seasons were favorable.

In modern societies, and especially our Western urban culture, the concept of possessing land or territory from which food can be obtained no longer applies. Instead, the guarantee of having enough to eat is dependent upon one's training, experience, and ability to keep employed.

In recent years with increasing affluence there has not been the anxiety or tension attached to procuring food that there once was. The present generation has scarcely known anything of the pangs of unemployment, soup lines, and long queues for a handout of food. But these were a part of the depression years, and those who lived through that awful era will never forget the terrible tension and worry of just getting enough to eat.

Nor has this anxiety actually diminished for many millions of less privileged people who scarcely know if their lips will taste food at all in the next twenty-four hours. Seldom do I bow my head to give thanks for the beautiful food before me without recalling the appalling hunger and starvation I have seen in other parts of the earth. It is a sobering thought. Sometimes one wonders just how long the Western world will be allowed to wallow in its wealth while other uncounted millions hover on the edge of famine. I have dealt at length with this subject in several of my other books, notably *Splendour from the Land*, so I shall not emphasize it here again.

The fact remains, though, that for some people, just the act of getting enough to eat represents anxiety, stress, worry, and concern.

In our Western world it is probably true to say that anxiety arises more over *what* we will eat or *how* it shall be prepared, than over merely procuring it. Evidence of this can be seen in numerous magazine articles, books, radio programs, TV shows, and general discussions of food and its preparation.

Among women, especially, this appears to be a never-ending tension in life—"What shall I cook?" This tension is heightened the moment a woman feels she is in competition with the cooking of her neighbors, friends, or relatives. No other single area of life seems to be so susceptible to the stress of trying hard to impress others as is the culinary field. Here competition puts people under enormous pressures to surpass. And it takes only one fallen cake for a cook's entire world to collapse in chaos and humiliation.

In saying this I do not intend to depreciate nor detract from the creative urge so strong in many people to produce appetizing meals. Both my first and second wives have been excellent cooks. They have known how to produce delicious meals with very modest ingredients. They have shown imagination and finesse in setting a fine table adorned with appetizing dishes. All of this is highly commendable and to be applauded. In fact, these efforts in the kitchen are genuinely appreciated.

The preparation of our food should be a pleasure and not a penance. It should have attached to it a certain joie de vivre and not the dread of disastrous failure. Too many cooks use their culinary skills as a coverup for failure in other directions. Naturally this only intensifies the dilemma and does them no good at all. For if they fail in their food, then they feel that they have failed completely. There is much more to life than eating, and to make food our sole and main preoccupation is to demonstrate our immaturity and lack of vision.

There is much, much more to life than merely worrying and fretting over what our next meal will be. Our Lord made this abundantly clear when He remarked rather bluntly, "Take no thought, saying, 'What shall we eat?' or, 'What shall we drink?' or, 'Wherewithal shall we be clothed?'" He was pointing out the secondary importance of food.

Practical advice on reducing the tensions that arise over our eating habits can be best summed up in two simple sentences. First, let us eat simply and unpretentiously. Secondly, let us eat wholesome food of the barest minimum.

The ancient Arabs had a marvelous motto which we can adopt as a rule for mealtime. It states simply, "Enough is a feast." It is so brief, yet it embraces a world of wisdom. Most of us eat far too much, far too often. As the old adage goes we literally "dig our graves with our teeth."

Considering the sedentary sort of lives led by millions of human beings, their food consumption is almost double what it needs to be. The result is a multitude of overweight, flabby, soft people who puff and perspire their way through life feeling only half alive.

This business of being really only half alive and in most cases carting around a disgraceful figure leads to even further tensions and anxieties. For one thing these people know they should feel better; they wonder why every task seems to require such a titanic effort; they fear the racing heartbeat that pounds in their veins as their overburdened heart struggles to cope with the extra load of flesh imposed upon it; they can sense all sorts of complications developing and they cringe at the thought they might be faced with coronary disease or some other bodily breakdown simply because they are overweight.

As if all these anxieties were not enough, their plight becomes even more pathetic because of their personal shame at feeling and looking like an overstuffed flour sack. They are ashamed of their figure or physique and try to hide it.

The answer to all of this is so simple and so straight-forward it is a joy to pass it on. Simply push yourself away from the table the moment you have had enough. Remember and repeat the old saying over and over: "Enough is a feast." It is that second serving of potatoes and gravy, that extra slice of bread, the additional scoop of ice cream, that add the extra pounds.

At first it may seem tough to turn away from the table not feeling absolutely full. But turn away one must if the tensions attached to food are to be tamed. In time you will discover a great, quiet dignity in saying, both to yourself and to your host, "I've had sufficient. Thank you." In no way does this detract from the delight of the meal, nor does it reflect upon the cooking. You may relish whatever has been served, but you have also learned that "enough is a feast."

In passing it needs to be emphasized that most of us eat much more than is required by our bodies to maintain them-selves in excellent condition. Just knowing this relieves some of the stress attached to eating. So many people are actually afraid that they and their families or guests are not getting enough to eat. In most cases the opposite is true. We all eat far too much.

There is a certain exhilaration and delightful release in learning to eat less. When we do, we suddenly begin to feel better; our bodies become more fit, our figures improve, and most of our fears evaporate with the vanishing fat from our frames.

Simplifying the diet is a much more difficult discipline than merely eating less. This is especially so if one has been accustomed to elaborate or extravagant diets.

It was not until my first wife had passed away and I was compelled to cook for myself that it dawned on me fully what splendid meals I had been conditioned to eat as a matter of course. One just gradually gets to the place where ample food of a wide variety becomes the accepted thing.

Suddenly I was thrust into a situation where I realized it

was no longer possible to lay a beautiful table. For one thing, I despised fussing with food. So there was really no alternative but to simplify my diet and find ways of preparing meals with a minimum of trouble.

Eventually it turned out that this was to become a great benefit. In the first place, because my food had previously been so tastefully prepared, I had been inclined to eat much more than I really needed. And just cutting down on the quantity consumed began to make me feel much more fit.

The second important change was to eat a wider variety of foods raw and uncooked. It was almost like discovering anew how delicious fresh fruit and vegetables could be without the bother of cooking or stewing them. I did take care to wash them well because so many are sprayed with chemicals and pesticides which are harmful to human health. In addition, it was reassuring to know that by eating them raw I was deriving maximum benefit from the minerals and vitamins in the produce; these otherwise would have been lost or destroyed in cooking.

In an amazing way, not only did this simple step soon improve my health, but it also set my mind free in a new dimension from the fret of worrying over food.

Perhaps one of the main practical problems to get around was potatoes, which constitute so great a part of most people's regular diet. Like Abraham Lincoln, I learned to eat these raw, sliced very thin, and lightly salted. It has been said this was his favorite dish to serve friends.

But over and beyond the few potatoes eaten this way, I turned to good, wholesome, whole-wheat bread. It can be used as an excellent substitute and is ever so much more nourishing because of its higher protein content.

An added advantage arising from the use of raw fruit, vegetables, and coarse, whole-wheat bread was the bowel regularity which resulted from consuming so much roughage. Constipation is recognized as one of the common maladies afflicting the human race. In fact it is the cause of much worry, anxiety, and distress in thousands of lives. Yet here lies a simple method of dealing with the difficulty.

One thing about eating a substantial amount of coarse or raw food is that one is more or less compelled to chew it well. It is, for instance, much more difficult to gulp down great chunks of hard, tough, uncooked carrot than it is a mouthful of the same vegetable soft-boiled. The necessity of having to chew food longer to reduce it to a finer form is an aid to digestion and of enormous benefit to the entire intestinal tract. It slows down the mealtime and eases our tensions.

There is a great mental benefit to be gained from regular mealtimes. There is something satisfying in knowing that our appetites will be assuaged at certain specific times. Too many people eat rather haphazardly, almost "on the run," and at all hours of the day or night.

Breakfast is the most abused meal in most homes. For literally millions of people it really does not exist at all. Snatching a quick cup of coffee, a cigarette, and, on occasion, a slice or two of toast is simply not eating intelligently. It is a downright insult to the body. Lack of proper nutrition puts the body under terrible strain and tension to meet the day's demands.

Far too many elaborate tests have been made to prove the necessity of eating a proper breakfast for me to elaborate on the point here. Suffice it to say that if an individual wishes to have vigor, vitality, energy, and a cheerful sense of well-being with which to face the day's work, the body must be fed to do it.

Even the average breakfast of fruit juice, toast, coffee, jam, and packaged cereal is too low in total nutrients for the day. At best, after an hour or two, energy output from such fare will fall off, leaving one tired, listless, grouchy, and tense.

The morning meal should contain, besides sugars and carbohydrates, some fats and a healthy helping of protein. This can be derived from bacon, ham, eggs, cheese, powdered skim milk, or even peanut butter. To prepare and eat such a meal may mean getting up half an hour earlier, but it is a sure guarantee that one will go through the day with zest and ease.

In the choice of a breakfast cereal, there are scores of manufactured products on the market. Few of these, despite their advertising blandishments, are worth their price. Yet most people detest cooked cereal. What then can one do? It was not until I visited Switzerland, the country of my forebears, that I stumbled on an amazing breakfast food whose formula is presented here.

Take raw rolled oats, add raisins, a sprinkle of cocoa, a few ground nuts if desired, and a dash of raw sugar. Stir the dry ingredients together, pour a little milk over them, and eat immediately.

When I brought this recipe home my family went wild over it and I have yet to find any children who don't relish this dish. It requires no cooking, no pots to clean up, no special preparation. Simply mix the dry ingredients together in a large container once or twice a month and spoon out whatever is required for the meal.

Speaking of sugar, most of us use far too much for our own good or that of our teeth. If we must use it, let the sweetening be as unrefined as possible, preferably the raw brown product or else honey. The same applies to wheat flour, rice, and any other processed foods which are milled or refined in any way.

Lunch, for many, is the most difficult meal of the day to deal with. Again and again women wail, "What can I get for lunch?" For cold, chilly weather a steaming bowl of wholesome soup with a few hearty sandwiches filled with protein pick-me-ups like salami, cheese, sardines, peanut butter, or cold meat is fine. A bit of fresh fruit is good for dessert. In warm, hot weather, the hot soups can be replaced by fresh salads. A tuna or salmon salad will help maintain protein levels if one does not want sandwiches.

The evening meal is traditionally the major meal of the day. The exception is on farms, where large noon meals are eaten. Irrespective of when this meal is taken, it too should be high in protein, with meat, fish, or fowl in generous supply, augmented again by an abundance of fresh vegetables and fruit.

In the life of the modern family, mealtime is one of the few occasions during the crowded day when the family can be united. Because of this the time given to eating should be doubly worthwhile.

The dining table should be placed in the most pleasant and brightest place in the home. The meal itself should be an orderly, quiet time during which the food is shared and eaten with pleasure and ease. Rush, hurry, and tension should be avoided. It is a good time for contented conversation and gentle good humor, all of which aid digestion. If possible, this atmosphere can be promoted by playing fine music softly.

Meals are no time for settling family feuds. Nor are they an appropriate place to pour contempt, ridicule, or criticism over others. Arguing and heated debates should be avoided. Instead, good cheer, gaiety, and genuine gratitude, both to the cook and God our Father, for delicious food can make mealtime a relaxing interlude during which the day's tensions are tamed.

Finally a few remarks are appropriate in this chapter about the purchase and production of food. Since the cost of food comprises one of the largest items in the family budget, it can cause a certain amount of real concern to the consumer. It was intimated earlier that because we of the West are now enjoying prosperous times, the old ogres of hunger, famine, and starvation do not stare us in the face as in former times. Despite this, living within one's budget can become a bit of a burden and a few suggestions are given here to help make ends meet.

First and foremost, do compare prices, not only between stores but between brands. It is amazing what savings there are to be had in shopping around a little.

Secondly, do not always insist on the best cut or the fanciest quality. You are really paying only for prestige, not more food value. Chuck steak is just as nourishing as sirloin and about half the cost.

Thirdly, invest your money in fresh produce and wholesome bread rather than canned produce and special, fancy pastries or baked goods. Dollar for dollar, you are getting better nutrition.

Fourthly, if you have transportation and the countryside

is not too far, make friends of some farmers and purchase farm produce from them directly. You will get better value and the joy of this firsthand contact with the land will help you live better. What is more, the trips out of town will help to relax and refresh you.

Last but by no means least, if you have a bit of ground, do try growing some of your own food. With a little care, determination, and labor it is fantastic how much food can be produced on a few square feet of soil. There are those who will argue that the cost of seed, fertilizers, sprays, and tools for the task more than offset the gains from one's garden. To a point this is true. Still it does not take into consideration the pleasure, relaxation, and joy which having a garden can produce in one's life. It is a tremendous tonic for tense and jaded people.

With the improvement of plant varieties and the introduction of dwarf fruit trees, the average backyard can supply an astonishing array of fruit and vegetables for the family table. What is more, because they can be picked fresh, you will vow they are the finest flavor you ever tasted.

All of these approaches to food can help to make life more of an adventure and less of a burden. There is indeed a certain element of adventure in trying to live well within one's means by use of wit, skill, and personal labor. The people who are really the most carefree are the ones who are busy at the "game of life." Getting something to eat means much more to them than running up an account at the corner store and carting home the packages. It embraces the many facets of finding good food at reasonable prices, in addition to the expenditure of one's own energy.

In fact it is all a bit of fun, and this in itself reduces the stress of struggling to survive.

5

Drinking

Drinking is not the sort of subject one can dismiss in a paragraph or two. It has become such an important part of social custom that it demands serious thought and study. Every effort will be made here to deal with it in a helpful and constructive manner. Too often the tendency is to try to brush aside the whole subject with a shrug of the shoulders. Instead I hope a better understanding of ourselves will become clear to the reader as we progress through this chapter.

The human body, like many animal bodies, is approximately 70 percent liquid or fluids. Every cell in the body contains some moisture. This fluid is absolutely essential for normal bodily functions. Moisture is a must for regular bodily metabolism. It maintains the turgidity of cells and is used in the various complex exchanges of food, minerals, vitamins, and wastes within the various systems of the body.

If we are to feel normal, well, and fit, the supply of water for the body must be replaced and replenished regularly. This offsets desiccation. Moisture is lost by the discharge of wastes in urine, feces, and perspiration. So it can be readily seen why the regular intake of liquids is so important. It is a simple, basic fact that without drinking we would die.

Dehydration of the body results in thirst. Thirst is in itself a form of tension. It is the signal that something is missing which needs to be replaced. The more intense the thirst, the greater is the need for restoring the level of liquids within the physical framework.

Fundamentally the only fluid required by the body is ordinary water. The cells of the body with its various complex organs are so remarkably adapted to their respective functions that they can use water for a great variety of purposes. It is perfectly possible for a person to maintain optimum health if he drinks nothing but clear, clean water.

This is a point which very few people fully comprehend. Why it should be so difficult for us to believe this is a bit of an enigma. One can imagine it is because, the world over, social custom dictates that drinking should include various sorts of brews and concoctions.

So deeply ingrained in the subconscious mind of many is the idea that they must drink a variety of beverages that they almost despise water as something inferior. In a sense one cannot blame them for this in some countries. For it is surprising how really difficult it is to find good clean water where wild animals, livestock, or even human populations have severely polluted streams, springs, rivers, or other water sources.

Even in some of our most enlightened Western countries, unless water supplies are chlorinated, the water may be dangerous to drink. And I have been in a number of countries where one dared to drink only boiled water. Now chlorinated water, boiled water, and water from questionable sources can be very poor stuff indeed to drink. It often has a repulsive flavor, it may appear murky, and because of its general unpalatability and health hazards it compels people to find refreshment in other drinks.

This reminds me of a very amusing anecdote. A friend of mine and his wife visited India. Because the lady was afraid of drinking polluted water, she determined to have nothing but coffee during the entire trip. In Delhi they purchased a newspaper with large headlines showing that the coffee merchants of the country were to be prosecuted for contaminating their product with powdered cow dung. When he read this, my friend, who has a keen sense of humor, turned to his wife and remarked, "Now, Nelly, what are you going to do?" There was a mischievous twinkle in his eye, but his wife was not to be deterred. "Me?" she shot back. "Why, I'm going to stop reading the newspapers!"

Of course, coping with contaminated water really is not this simple. As human populations proliferate upon the planet, good, clean, clear water will become an increasingly scarce commodity. As it is, most people in great cities now have to be content with chlorinated water. Some of it is awful, especially for those who have been accustomed to drink from clear mountain streams, pure springs, or clean, cool wells.

But it is enough to say that for general physical fitness one should see to it that several glasses of water are drunk each day. Drinking adequate amounts of water aids digestion, assists bowel regularity, and keeps the body in excellent condition. Very often those people with the clearest and best complexions are regular water drinkers. Delicious water is a delight to drink. There is real pleasure in drinking cool, clean water.

It will be noted that I have not used the term *pure water*. Really there is no such thing. The best of water if examined under a microscope will be found to contain some foreign matter or even numerous harmless microorganisms. But clean, cool, clear water can be had in most places with a little effort.

It is neither desirable nor beneficial to drink water too cold. It only chills the intestinal tract and puts it under stress.

If one can learn to be content with water as the main drink in life it is downright surprising how it simplifies things. Often I have said to friends who tried to force me into drinking a lot of tea, coffee, or other brewed beverages, "But why? Why take a satisfactory substance—water—and boil the oxygen out of it, then add sugar (which we seldom need), and milk, an extra expense, plus the stimulant that must be purchased?" This takes time, trouble, and effort to make, not to mention the bother of buying all the additional ingredients.

This is a point in case where much of the strain and anxiety connected with an everyday custom can be reduced by simplifying our tastes. If we are to be realistic about relieving ourselves of much of the tension in life we have to be bold enough to be different and reduce some of our habits to utter simplicity.

There are certain circles in which the drinking of tea or coffee and the time and details devoted to the custom constitute an appalling social conformity. And it simply must be admitted that conformity implies pressures and tensions upon individuals who comply simply because they feel they must. In other words, they are afraid not to do the accepted thing. In many cases they may actually despise tea or coffee or what have you, yet they take it lest they offend. This is foolish. Why live under fear of offending? Why not be bold enough and brave enough simply to say, "If you have a glass of water I would prefer that, thanks!" And smile as you do it.

By this one does not mean to be mean or rude or difficult. It is simply being oneself. There are times, especially if we are very weary, chilled, or limp after long hours of work, that a cup of coffee or tea is a delightful pick-me-up. It is surprising what a strong stimulus they supply. At the same time they provide a most pleasant interlude.

Yet it is this same content of caffein or tannin which becomes the crutch upon which millions of men and women rely to get them through the average day. Little do most of them realize that they pay a double price for this dependence. First they must purchase and prepare the beverages, and secondly they place their entire nervous system under tension and stress. If this were not so, doctors and athletic coaches would not recommend discontinuation of these drinks, coffee in particular, for patients or athletes whose bodies are under strain.

This is not to condemn the use of these home-brewed

beverages. They have a place in our lives. But far too many of us become tense, nervous, irritable, and unwell because the tea or coffee pot is used much, much more than it ought to be for simple, carefree living.

When I first met the lady who was to become my second wife, she was an inveterate coffee drinker. Coming from northern Europe where this custom is taken for granted, she naively assumed there could be no harm in the habit. It was very noticeable that she was edgy and inclined to be tense and irritable at times. Little by little I prevailed upon her to give up the habit. What is more, if she simply had to have a cup of coffee, I suggested use of the decaffeinated brands. The change in her general well-being, serenity, and cheerfulness has been beautiful to watch. Even she herself admits now how much more relaxed and free of fretful tension she is.

Apart from this it is fairly common knowledge that tea and coffee contribute to sleeplessness. They are stimulants, not soporific drinks. In some people they also aggravate the kidneys and interfere with the normal discharge of wastes from the body.

If one feels that water alone is not good enough, and there are some who seem unable to enjoy a glass or two of water, milk is better than most beverages. Milk that is truly delicious to drink is often much harder to come by than even decent water. In some countries it has become a distinctly expensive drink. It is not easy to keep fresh without refrigeration. It has the great advantage of being both a drink and a food. Whole milk and skim milk are decidedly nutritious. For adults and children, powdered skim milk is a high protein food which can be added to the diet. It is readily stored, it keeps well, it is simple to prepare, and it provides a balanced food supply.

Perhaps most important, from the standpoint of this book, at least, is the soothing effect of milk on tense people. Those who are inclined to worry, fret, or suffer from tension that might even lead to stomach or duodenal ulcers can do no better than drink plenty of milk. The moment one senses strain or anxiety with its attendant twinges in the torso, he should enjoy a glass of milk. If an overactive mind throbs and churns over some complex problem at night, the anxiety can often be quickly tamed with a cool, tall glass of milk.

As with water, so with milk; there are some people who find it difficult to drink straight milk by itself. For such there are other beverages like hot chocolate, Postum, and Ovaltine which can be taken. These are nutritious and will insure that some milk is drunk.

Then there comes the whole range of so-called soft drinks. These need no particular comment except one or two things which some readers may not realize. First is the fact that most of them have a very undesirable effect on teeth. If you are concerned about decay and dental bills, then leave them alone. Secondly, they have absolutely no food value. It cannot be denied that they provide a pleasant break during trying weather. But water or milk can be just as refreshing. If one is afflicted with an upset stomach, ordinary ginger ale, 7-Up, or Pepsi can quickly remedy the situation because of the soda content. By and large, however, it seems most soft drinks are poor substitutes indeed for milk or water.

When we consider intoxicating drinks, the whole subject becomes much more complex. Nonetheless it deserves some discussion simply because in many homes and many lives it is a question of major importance that deeply affects the entire family.

It has never ceased to amaze me that the human race, irrespective of man's geographical location and state of civilization, has mastered the art of brewing intoxicating drinks. The variety of materials used is quite astonishing. It may be anything from grapes to guavas, from barley to bananas, from wild honey to coconuts, from dates to dandelions. The world around in every society man has devised a method of making a drink on which it is possible to become inebriated.

It would be quite unfair and unjust to assert that alcoholic beverages are brewed just so people can get drunk. They are not. There are quite literally millions of families and millions of homes where the daily use of wine or some other such drink is used at the table for an appetizer or an agreeable adjunct to the meal. Likewise, there are many, many people who have mastered the ability to enjoy a modest drink at the end of the day's activities without wanting in any way to get drunk.

But "spirits" have the name, in part at least, simply because they do tend to soothe tension and raise our spirits. They are referred to by another friend of mine as the "Oh, be joyful!" drinks, which in itself indicates their capacity for relaxing a person and putting him in a more agreeable frame of mind.

This reminds me of an elderly gentleman who was having his baggage inspected by a customs officer. When asked what his suitcase contained, he replied, "Just clothes!" Opening the case, the officer was amazed to find a bottle of whiskey in the bottom. "I thought you said this suitcase contained only clothes!" he growled, holding up the bottle. "I did," the old gentleman replied, "That in your hand is my nightcap."

This anecdote points up how important a wee drink can be to some before bed. Others have a bottle of brandy on hand which is used more for pick-me-ups and medicinal purposes than anything else.

What we have said so far is perhaps the best that can be put forward for the regular use of intoxicants. Like the drinking of tea or coffee, the use of cocktails has been long accepted as a social part of living. Whether or not one is prepared to be different and not drink socially is a personal matter.

It is not always easy to refuse a drink. A certain stigma is attached to the thought of being an abstainer. Nevertheless it is not something of which to be ashamed. If it is grounded on deep personal convictions about the dangers of drink then it is surely to be commended and admired. For when all is said and done the misuse of intoxicating drinks does enormous damage. Not until one has personally had to face the consequences of alcoholism in all of its devious forms does the truth of this statement come home. The e are far too many who try to laugh off the evils of liquor. The word *evils* is used without apology, for the destructive effects of liquor are apparent in too many places and too many lives to treat it lightly.

The utter tragedy of intoxicating drink is the fact that no one really knows whether or not he can handle it. I have friends who all their lives have been only moderate drinkers. They never wasted much money on alcohol; what little they did spend was well repaid in the pleasure they derived from an occasional drink.

On the other hand I have had firsthand acquaintance with many people for whom alcohol was an absolute curse. The appetite for this atrocious stuff was so insatiable that it produced terrible havoc and ruin in both their own lives and that of their families.

It cannot be denied that drink in itself can ease tension, relieve anxiety, and relax a person. Its very ability to do this is what makes it so desirable. But to use it as an escape is extremely dangerous. Alcohol is the great escape for many people, but it is escaping from one area of anxiety into an even worse situation. One may scoff at this statement, but it remains a sober fact. People in the grip of alcoholism find themselves in a dreadful fever of ferment. Those of us who have had to counsel and help such people know all too well the terrible penalty exacted by drink. Not only does it destroy the individual himself, it can exhaust his financial resources, imperil his mind, ruin his family, wreck his home, and demolish his career.

Because of this young people are urged to stay away from intoxicating drinks. It is not good enough for anyone to say, "Oh, never mind, you can handle it." No one really can be absolutely sure. The line between a mere social drinker and an alcoholic is so very obscure and so unknown that many have passed over it without realizing the peril in which they were placing themselves.

It has been shown that for every six young ladies who ever take a drink at least one becomes an alcoholic. For men, the percentage is somewhat lower. Still the danger is so appalling it is better to avoid it altogether. The courage and boldness of those who abstain for the benefit of their own bodies and the welfare of their families is to be admired.

In fairness to all concerned it must be pointed out that the very use of alcohol itself creates its own peculiar tensions.

First of all there is the cost of purchasing spirits. Money spent this way puts an extra strain on family finances. If there is heavy drinking, it may well mean that funds which should be used for nourishing food or clothing are spent instead on liquor. Moreover, should only one or two members of a family be drinkers and the others not, friction and ill will are created. If drunkenness becomes a factor in the home, it generates deep tensions and anxieties among the various members.

In advanced cases of alcoholism the sufferer is under constant and terrifying tension. There is the ever-present fear that liquor may not be available. There is the anxiety about possibly losing a job or not being promoted. The specter of bankruptcy and deep indebtedness hangs over the head. There are deep personal pain, shame, and a desire to do better, but inability to beat the bottle. And finally, in very advanced stages the torture and agony of delirium tremens subject the sufferer to excruciating tensions.

From this it must surely be seen that in truth drinking can involve a delusion. Thinking that one can tame tension by taking a drink is very often taking the first step on the path to self-destruction. It is a terrible risk. It is not the sort of gamble any person should take who respects himself or his home.

Happily there are other sure, sound, and very satisfactory ways of taming our tensions. Let us do the wise and intelligent thing.

6

Doctors and Drugs

A number of years ago an article on medicine as practiced throughout the world attracted special attention. It pointed out that in China, doctors were paid to keep the public from getting ill. The emphasis has been just the opposite in the West, where physicians are paid to get us well, after we have become sick. In other words, prevention of disease was much more important to the Chinese than the diagnosis and remedy of any illness that might overtake the patient.

In reality, it is this same philosophy (prevention is much better than any cure) which runs through this whole book. The great majority of illnesses and diseases which afflict people can be prevented. Common sense in our way of living, combined with simplicity of life and a few secrets on taming tension, can help reduce illness to a minimum. In saying this I am not implying that we shall forever be free from all sickness. That is absurd. But men and women can live reasonably normal, healthy, productive lives without depending on either doctors or drugs.

It is astonishing how many people literally lean on medical

practitioners and their prescriptions to pull them through life. It is not altogether clear whether the sort of individual who is forever running to the doctor or a drugstore needs physical attention or moral support. More often than not it is probably the latter.

It is simply a fact that many individuals, and more especially women, often find the listening ear and the sympathetic attention they instinctively crave in the doctor's office. Nor do they seem to mind paying a very high price for this individual attention. Combined with this is the utter and complete confidence with which they place themselves under the practitioner's control.

Men and women who under other circumstances in life exercise the greatest caution and wisdom will, when it comes to doctors, do anything they say. It is almost as if the ancient magic and superstition attached to the powers of medicine men or native witch doctors have persisted to the present. Many medical practitioners are well-nigh deified as though they could do no wrong nor ever commit an error.

This same mysterious, almost magical aura is extended right on through to the writing out of special prescriptions in symbols and language no laymen can decipher. The doctor prepares a profound piece of paper for a pharmacist who, in turn, perpetuates the secret spell by slipping into his back room to concoct the special remedy from the bewildering array of strange ingredients on his shelves. To top it off, both doctor and druggist charge a fine fee for their services. The patient, meanwhile, departs feeling sure his or her very life has been spared, convinced the medication will do marvels.

It is utterly impossible to guess how many millions of dollars are spent annually this way. The figure would be of astronomical proportions, most of it paid out to procure a little peace of mind.

I have no personal grudge against doctors. Several doctors are among my finest and most respected friends for whom I have great affection and admiration. They are sincere, honest, and well-educated men. They do their best to bring a real measure of relief to those who come to them. They use all the skill of their profession and the most modern techniques of the times to help mend the bodies of their patients.

But that is as far as they can go. They themselves admit frankly that they are after all only fallible human beings. They are just as likely to make errors and misjudgments as anyone else. They can, in some cases, do no better than arrive at calculated guesses at what is really wrong. They are subject to the same bodily weariness and mental strain as the rest of us, during which times they, too, can be less than 100 percent efficient. They work in conjunction with nurses, hospital attendants, druggists, and other practitioners who may often be less competent, less efficient, less conscientious than themselves. Because of all this the possibilities that their remedies or procedures may not produce the desired results are multiplied.

But over and above this there are many, many doctors who are not as dedicated, not as sincere, not as skilled as my special friends.

In addition, literally hundreds of tons of tranquilizers, sedatives, and other medications are prescribed and consumed annually in the search for serenity. Yet at best in all of this there is only partial help in medicine for taming tension permanently.

Actually it is often tension itself which is the tyrant that produces the aches and pains in the patient. Treating these symptoms is not to treat the cause of the complaint. In fact many medical men will be honest enough and brave enough to tell us that our problems are really not organic or physical at all. They lie in the realm of mind and spirit, a region no amount of treatment with drugs or surgery can ever hope to help.

Because of all this it is important to realize that every little twinge of pain or obscure ache arising in our anatomies is not cause for deep concern. If we can learn to live with ourselves and laugh at many of our own silly fears, there will be less reason to run to the doctor or druggist for every little pain. There can be no doubt at all that the mere thought of doctors, hospitals, and treatment is enough to arouse and intensify tension in some people. Nor do we help ourselves by believing that we are sure to die unless we dash off to the doctor.

As intimated in an earlier chapter, the body has an enormous capacity to heal and mend itself, given half a chance. Its chances of doing this normally and readily are often reduced when we resort to drugs or even surgery, which in many cases only complicate the illness.

Somehow when all is said and done there is such a thing as having a serene outlook of quiet confidence in our bodies. Of course, there are emergencies which suddenly arise; there are accidents; there are acute complications which demand the attention of a doctor, but in the average lifetime these may be quite rare, leaving us to lead healthy lives the rest of the time.

Another point to be borne in mind is that unless one has adequate medical coverage, doctor bills, hospital fees, and prescription costs can be paralyzing. Some people spend years of their lives trying to pay medical bills. This in itself can impose a terrible strain on both the patient and his family. So again the simple comment is, "Keep away from the doctors and druggists if you can possibly manage it." In the long run it will be easier on both your pocketbook and your peace of mind.

It is naturally wise to have a regular checkup, just as it is prudent to have one's automobile greased and serviced, and the oil changed regularly. But to press the simile a step further, we realize that almost any mechanic could find half a dozen faults with our cars right now which he would insist need correction. In exactly the same manner, if we even so much as hint that this or that may need attention in our bodies, a doctor could diagnose half a dozen difficulties or diseases which need his care.

It is necessary to exercise a certain amount of good common sense in this connection. Just as an automobile if given reasonable care will keep running well with little or no trouble, so will our bodies. Given even a modicum of attention and sensible care, they can carry on and function free of serious breakdown.

There are a few simple suggestions which we pass on here

for what they are worth. They have to do with common complaints.

For many, many years colds were a real curse to our family. Every winter was a long succession of one horrible head cold after another, sometimes settling down into throat and chest with attendant complications. Then we read about using vitamin C (ascorbic acid). The results were so immediate and so effective it was like sheer magic. Now, whenever there is the slightest sign of a cold coming on we simply swallow several tablets of vitamin C pills and the cold is arrested.

It is not generally known that it is safe to take very large dosages of vitamin C. Any excess in the body is passed off harmlessly in the urine. In cases of massive infection as much as 3000-4000 units in a twenty-four-hour period can be taken to forestall complications. This applies especially to influenza and other minor fevers. Just knowing that there is such a simple and inexpensive remedy available for so many maladies removes much of the anxiety otherwise attached to illness.

The same applies to the use of calcium to counteract tension and stress. It may seem hard to credit but the regular use of calcium can actually change a disposition. Instead of being tense and edgy, one's inner nervous system can be calmed by calcium. Calcium is also helpful in reducing stress from pain and suffering. To be most effective, it requires large doses of Vitamin D to be properly absorbed in the body.

Vitamin D is best absorbed by exposing ourselves to sunlight with all of its benefits. But in cold, dull, gray weather it can be derived from cod-liver oil extracts or other pills.

Then there is vitamin E. It is thought that two factors play a large part in preventing the ravages of cancer in the body. One is freedom from tension or stress and the other is ample supplies of vitamin E. Any person who is constantly under strain is more open and susceptible to suffering from cancer than someone who is calm and relaxed. By the same measure anyone who is well supplied with vitamin E in the body is less likely to succumb to cancer than is someone who is deficient in it.

The commonest source of this rather rare vitamin is wheat-germ oil. Capsules containing this ingredient are fairly inexpensive and if taken regularly are an excellent investment for healthy living. Both mv present wife and I have had a record of cancer, but by taking these pills regularly, enjoy excellent health with few signs of cancer complications. Again this suggestion is merely passed on to help reduce the pressure which the dread of this disease can impose on people.

Before concluding this chapter on drugs and doctors a few brief comments should be made about both drug addiction and smoking, the latter being a socially accepted form of addiction.

All the evils which attend the use of heroin, morphine, LSD, marijuana, and nicotine have been so widely publicized in the press, on radio, and on TV that it would scarcely seem necessary to discuss them here.

Basically the paramount question is, "Why do people use drugs? Why seek relief, or escape, in these drugs?"

The answers, generally speaking, though diverse, can be best summed up in two simple statements. First, those who turn to drugs do so out of a sense of wanting to belong, to be accepted as one of a social group. This is especially true of teen-agers; it is in the teen-age years that addiction generally starts. There is a fear of being different. There is the pressure to conform and be one of the crowd. And so to be "in," they give in.

Secondly, there is a turning to drugs as a form of finding security. The sensation of being calmed or quieted or lifted out of the dilemma of difficult circumstances has a strong appeal. Because modern society exerts so many pressures on people, desire for escape from the tensions, stress, and unhappiness of home or work induces people to turn to drugs.

From the foregoing it will be noted that the greatest contributing causes of drug addiction are fears, anxieties, tensions, and stress. And it is the taming of these tensions that this book is all about. It is unfair to anyone to say, *"Don't use drugs!!"* unless some far better method of taming tension can be given.

It is my ardent hope that this book will be read by young people as well as older folk. It has been written in the high hope that it will get a hearing with teen-agers as well as older people. And I again emphasize the need to treat our bodies with great self-respect, honor, dignity, and consideration. When we come to appreciate their own wondrous ability to mend and maintain themselves when given proper care, we will realize what a dishonor it is to subject them to drugs.

Besides all the obvious evils and disadvantages of drug addiction such as lung cancer, impaired health, damaged brains, and weakened physiques there remains one great difficulty seldom mentioned in the popular press. It is guilt. I have had sufficient counseling contact with drug addicts to realize how they literally recoil from themselves. In a deep, disquieting way they feel a sense of shame and personal revulsion to which they will seldom admit openly. They know they have betrayed their bodies and abused their minds. This becomes a psychological block that they can hardly ever handle without help. It is a living hell. They want out, but don't know how. How much better never to have taken the first smoke or the first shot or the first taste.

7

Sexual Life

So much has been written about sex and love that one almost fears to add a few more lines to the mass of material. But because the sexual impulses are so powerful and so important to normal bodily behavior they simply must be dealt with here.

It was stated in an earlier chapter that next to the two primal drives of holding territory and finding food, that of reproduction is the most important. Recognizing this to be so clears away much of the basic misunderstanding about the behavior between men and women.

When we simply recognize that we are designed to reproduce ourselves much of the mystery and apprehension surrounding sex can be reduced. Far too many people take the approach that somehow sexual impulses are something strange, something added, something apart from the normal functions of the body. Because of this perverted view, a great deal of distortion surrounds the subject. For many it is as if there were real disgrace attached to the reproductive processes.

Actually just the opposite should be the case. One may be a bit bewildered by the general attitude held towards certain parts of the human anatomy. For example, some are at a loss to understand why a lady's cheeks or hands or ankles should be considered worthy of such special esteem while her breasts or buttocks are often demeaned or ridiculed. Surely they are all part and parcel of the same person, fashioned and formed by the same incredible physiological processes and therefore deserving of the same dignified respect.

Why a man's reproductive organs should be considered repulsive while we admire his massive chest or bulging biceps is a bit bewildering. The total body in its entirety should be looked upon as an object of integrity, strength, and virility. A great deal of false modesty is attached to concealing certain parts of the anatomy, while in fact we often turn around and deliberately emphasize these very parts by our dress. It is all a bit hypocritical and somewhat of a farce.

If one has been reared in such a way that there is a stigma attached to the sexual organs, it is difficult to view them in any other way. In fact this unhealthy attitude in itself gives rise to peculiar inhibitions, fears, and anxieties which in themselves are hard to allay. One is afraid of undue exposure, of being seen undressed, of changing clothes, of all sorts of peculiar tensions.

The only possible, sensible, simple way to deal with these feelings is to take a totally different outlook on the body. It is a splendid physical form concerning which we are fully entitled to take a happy and relaxed attitude without apology.

This point cannot be overemphasized. It is the only sure and proper path to wholesome sexual attitudes. If we insist on or persist in the assumption that there is something essentially sinister or debasing about our bodies we are bound to have tension and trouble in this area of life. In the very nature of things human beings fear that which they suppose or imagine to be injurious. So, if they believe their own bodies are to be feared, they will do just that and actually dread their own design.

This is especially true of young people. As they approach

adolescence and pass through their unpredictable teens, there is almost a terror attached to their sexual life. Nor are their fears allayed if their parents, friends, or casual companions fan the flames of foreboding. Feelings of fantastic insecurity, unloveliness, and ungainliness sweep over them. Terrible tensions are built up around the body and its "peculiar" behavior. Anxiety develops over trying to prove one's prowess as a lover. The great gulf between dreams of accomplishment and the petty frustrations of puppy love becomes an agony of suspense and wondering what life and love are all about. No wonder so many youths are in a continuous fever of ferment.

A great part of this is due to the fact that many simply do not understand basic sexual behavior. It is very important for us to realize that not only is sexual intercourse absolutely essential for the reproduction of the race, but also this very basic function is something of supreme beauty and great dignity. This is not just a lofty, hypothetical statement. It is a fundamental fact. Admittedly, few people have truly discovered this truth for themselves. It is astonishing how the masses never discover the exaltation and inspiration inherent in the realm of sex. But this in no way diminishes the truth.

It is the secret hope of most men and women that somehow they will discover deep meaning and significance in their sexual life. Unfortunately, few do. Instead their dreams are not fulfilled; they feel that they have been frustrated in their finest aspirations; and, consequently, sex becomes a sordid thing. Worse still, this builds up stress, tension, and anxiety that can be most destructive.

If we are to tame the tensions which otherwise are bound to arise around sex, we must appreciate that the completion of this bodily function is more than just a biological act. I have included sex in this part of the book simply because it is generally regarded as a purely physical function. But it is not. It may be in a dog or a donkey, but it is not in human beings. It involves our minds, our emotions, and our spirits.

It is precisely at this point that the majority of people run into trouble. They attempt to treat something which involves their entire person as though it were merely a bodily function pertaining to just the physical portion of their makeup.

The very reason why sex has become such a sordid, sour part of many people's lives is that it has been regarded as something insignificant. Too often it is treated too lightly. It is looked upon almost as a game. For many it is nothing more than a self-centered way to satisfy selfish impulses. Little wonder that so many find it well-nigh repulsive, or at best something to put up with.

We are forced, therefore, to lift this subject out of the narrow realm of the physical into a much wider one, examining it from the standpoint of the whole person. And this naturally leads to a brief discussion of what "love" really is. For it is quite impossible to lift sexual behavior to the lofty level of noble living without true love.

There may be intense physical passion, there may be the most erotic techniques, there may be momentary ecstasy, but these alone will leave behind only a legacy of lust, not love.

Love in its most basic form is simply *self-lessness*. This is in contradistinction to *self-ishness*. A great deal which poses and passes as love in sexual relationships is not love but its exact antithesis. Instead of sex becoming a sublime act of *selflessness*, far more often it is the exact opposite, utter *selfishness*.

Until one can see the validity of the statements made in the preceding paragraph, there will be deep and terrible tension over sex. Even the most hardened man or woman who exploits a member of the opposite sex in order to gratify his or her own selfish impulses suffers stress because of it. It may appear on the surface that their behavior can be shrugged off with a laugh, but deep down inside they are aware that they are being not only self-destructive but exceedingly selfish in their treatment of another human being. This is simply because normal sexual behavior is not intended as a means of taking unfair advantage of another. It is intended rather to be a deeply meaningful act in which two people, devoted to each other, seek thereby to show their utmost concern and affection for each other. This concern finds fulfillment in each giving the other the utmost enjoyment and satisfaction.

The primary and overriding impulse which should govern each partner is not, "What can I get out of this?" but rather, "What can I do and give my mate in these magic moments to make them utterly sublime?" Total self-giving is the essence of satisfactory sexual behavior. And this embraces much more than merely giving of my body—it includes also giving my entire being.

Because so many individuals try to limit their sexual functions to just a physical act they are poorer than they think. Not only are they cheating their mate, but they are also cheating themselves. There is something very destructive and very debasing about this sort of behavior. And it explains why, despite all the propaganda of a permissive society to the contrary, sexual relationships outside the bonds of devotion to a "true life mate" are never satisfying.

I have used the term *true life mate* for lack of a better one. For the sad and inescapable fact is that society is burdened by millions of marriages which, though they be legally valid, are not made up of true life mates. Men and women may live together in matrimony but not be true life mates. There may actually be intense hostility between them. They are husband and wife but not true life mates.

By the same measurement there are millions of people in our present permissive society who, even though living together but without the bonds of marriage, are not true life mates. More often than not they are intensely selfish people. In order to satisfy their sexual impulses they find someone upon whom they can impose themselves without assuming even the basic responsibilities of a marriage. Very frequently they maintain this sort of liaison only as long as it serves their selfish ends, whereupon they discard their companion.

Men especially are guilty of this conduct. That they can find girls gullible enough to go along with it is surprising. I say this because most women do have some sort of deep intuition of what is good for them. The craze for equality, even in so-called sexual relations, will lead only to misery. For ultimately it is the woman who pays the appalling price of hating herself if she has shared herself with anyone but a true life mate.

The reason for this is fairly simple to understand, but it is astonishing how few men or women ever grasp it. Let me explain:

A man's primary role in sexual behavior is twofold. First he cultivates the girl of his choice. This includes courting her, complimenting her, giving her to understand she is of special significance to him, in short, setting the scene for the next step. The second stage involves preliminary love play— caresses, kisses, and arousing the woman to the point where impregnation is possible. With that accomplished the drama for him is over and done. He has fulfilled his part and is satisfied.

The woman's role, in the normal course of events, without taking precautions against pregnancy, is much more complex and of much greater duration. First, she reacts to the courting and attentions of the man either by flirting, being coy, or responding with her utmost feminine charms. Secondly, if the setting suits her and she is desirous of cementing the relationship she will enjoy petting, kissing, and other intense intimacies.

But unlike the man, who at this point is all done, her role has really just gotten well under way. That is, if she desires to experience complete and total fulfillment as a whole woman. She will dream of and deeply desire conception. Her entire being has been aroused to receive the male sperm, which, when it unites with her own ovum, will set in motion a whole new chain of events. There will follow pregnancy and all the enormous implications of producing another member of the race. After this nine-month interval of pent-up hopes and aspirations for her offspring there is the suspense of childbirth. The actual parturition and giving of birth to a baby is just one of a whole series of dramatic developments totally unfamiliar to the man.

As if this were not enough, then come lactation and the nursing of the newborn infant. As she holds the tiny bundle to her breasts she is keenly aware that only now has she fully realized all the profound purposes for which she, as a woman, was made. Writing this as a man, one who is a father of children, I am very keenly aware that no man can possibly enter into these experiences and all that they mean to a woman. So in short I say again that the role of proper fulfillment in sexual matters is infinitely more complex and extended for the woman than it is for the man.

Because of this if a girl gives herself to anyone other than a true life mate with whom she intends to reproduce the race, she knows she is cheating herself. If she indulges in sex without complete fulfillment of her feminine role in life, she is haunted by a peculiar stress and strain arising from a foreshortening of her feminine role. She feels frustrated and undone.

The man, meanwhile, who refuses to commit himself to the woman as a true life mate knows that he is betraying her. Of course, there are exceptions to this. Either he or she may be unable physically to procreate. Or they may be aware that they are emotionally unfit for parenthood. Or some other overriding reason may be present to prevent reproduction.

In this case the two partners should have a complete and comprehensive understanding on the matter. And if, in spite of these deterrents, it is possible for the woman to feel fulfilled by playing only a part of her total role, connubial bliss is possible. But such sublime satisfaction can come only when both people have given themselves to each other in the mutual understanding that they are indeed true life mates, that they intend to stay together through thick and thin, that they have each chosen the other as the supreme object of their mortal affection, that this sovereign exercise of their wills in a specific choice involves an attitude of complete and selfless love for the other.

Within the bonds of marriage and in mutual harmony, such soul mates or true life mates are bound to enjoy ecstasy in their sexual behavior. In part this is because of the utter confidence each has in the other. It is also because each can relax in the knowledge and assurance that his or her companion has only the other's best interests at heart.

When two people decide to share life together for good, in this spirit of total selflessness, then the groundwork has been laid for noble and lofty sexual intercourse. Gone from all sexual behavior are the fears, stress, and strains which otherwise surround sex. In their place there is an aura of light-hearted, carefree joy in this lovely part of life.

Without total and complete commitment, sex degenerates into little more than a pathetic sort of performance. Both partners know instinctively and deeply that they are defrauding each other. They become jaded and soon the edge of ecstasy has left their relationship. One or the other wearies of the experience and sooner or later jettisons the companion in a joyless termination. It is all a bit tragic, but very prevalent in our twentieth-century society.

Under the strain and stress of such false and shallow relationships it is well-nigh impossible to have either peace of mind or serenity of spirit. This is even more tormenting when these are the very objects sought in sexual behavior.

On the other hand, when a man and woman are completely committed the whole picture is at once altered. Suddenly the fear of failure, apprehension over a possible breakup, and the stress of not truly trusting one's mate are gone.

It is in this atmosphere of quiet confidence and mutual trust that love can grow. This may not mean that right from the start a couple will be perfectly compatible in their sexual life, but it does mean that they have every chance and hope of becoming so.

To find and give each other the ultimate in physical satisfaction is more than mere physical union. It is really an art of the highest form. It is the essence of sharing. It is seeing to it that every look, every kiss, every caress, every touch has sincere meaning that fosters affection and warmth.

If each is desirous that the other enjoy the experience to the utmost, nothing will be done to discourage or dismay the mate. Nor will there be any sense of fear or foreboding. Rather, man and woman come to each other in openhearted abandon. A spontaneous joy engulfs them as they rise together to new heights of ecstasy.

There should not be a sense of rush or haste or hurry in such sublime interludes. Experience and time and patience will show each how to encourage the other in total self-abandonment. And by the same token, time will be taken to insure that both obtain the same degree of delight during their ecstatic embraces.

Finally there should be the sublime sensation of reaching the highest pinnacle of perfect union as together they are enfolded in a complete climax. Accompanying this stupendous thrill is a sweet and satisfying sense of delicious release. All the pent-up energies, all the vigorous vitality, flow out in a surging flood of joyous fulfillment.

What I have written is not theory. It is not an ideal never attained. It is not just sentimental imagery. It is not romantic daydreaming. It is the very best of sexual behavior. It may not come easily. It may not come quickly. But it can come to any couple determined to have it.

It will be found that few bodily functions can do as much to dispel stress and anxiety and tension as sexual intercourse between two devoted people. It is a certain cure for the concern, worries, and petty irritations which plague so many people. Somehow, lying in one's lover's arms makes the whole world a better place.

The Chinese have a very ancient proverb which says, "Happiness is someone to love, something to do, and something to hope for." To a large degree all three of these very special ingredients are bound up in noble and fine sexual behavior. For the true life mate is the one to love. And if there is rich fulfillment to be found within the framework of love, then having sexual intercourse can be one of the most wonderful things in all the world to do. Added to all of this are the confident hope and knowledge that with each experience the ecstasy becomes more rewarding and more satisfying.

What has been written here has been written in utter sincerity and open honesty. If from personal, private experience I did not know it to be both possible and practical I would not advocate it.

Sexual behavior of this kind lends enormous excitement to

life. It brings a keen sense of well-being to people. It banishes boredom and the slow grinding frustrations of unfulfilled lives. It adds zest to one's outlook. It instills an enormous sense of quiet serenity in the life. It eases all the tensions and anxieties attached to our sexual lives. Above all it fills men and women with deep joy and great composure.

Such a secret source of strength and tranquility should not be abused. As with eating, "enough is a feast." But for those who have learned to love deeply and live richly in this realm there is a treasure house of tranquility which no money or medicine can ever secure. This is a dimension of life devised by God our Father for the delight of His children.

PART TWO

Mental and Emotional Life

8

The Mind and Emotions

In the same way that physical ailments may cause us mental stress and anxiety, so the mind, if disturbed and under tension, can cause physical suffering. The fine line between physical and emotional suffering is sometimes so obscure and ill-defined that it is well-nigh impossible to distinguish one from the other. Even the most expert physicians are sometimes unable to diagnose where the difficulty lies. Some people experience intense pain in their bodies when in fact there is nothing organically wrong. The suffering is but a bodily expression of stress or tension which may have its seat in the mind or emotions.

To put it in its most simple, straightforward terms, we are obliged to say that the total person is a most complex organism. The ordinary human being is an astoundingly complicated interaction of body, mind, and spirit. And when we come to deal with and discuss the mind of man we are faced with all the difficulties of dealing in abstracts. These include such intangible attributes as emotions, attitudes, sentiments, memory, and disposition.

This book is not intended to be a technical treatise on the mind. There are innumerable excellent works on both psychology and psychiatry. There is no intention here to handle these subjects in either a profound or professional way. Rather, once again, the aim is to share with the reader a few simple insights into the subject.

I recall very clearly a most challenging and helpful conversation with a very distinguished doctor about twenty-five years ago. It was just about the time that I was starting to do serious writing of books. He said to me then, "Phillip, the greatest difficulty and the most formidable challenge of this century is communication. We have all sorts of very skilled and very highly trained technical people, but precious few who can convey their knowledge to others. The great need of our generation is to take our technical know-how and translate it into simple language that the average layman can grasp."

I never forgot what he said. In all my writing over the ensuing years the main aim and objective has been to try to state useful information in such a way that the most untutored can grasp it. At times I have been criticized for the simplicity of my style and lack of so-called scientific approach. But no one has ever accused me of lacking sincerity or integrity in my endeavor to convey a message to the reader. Many very profound and scientific works fail simply because they are too technical. So, if, in the pages which follow, I deal with the mind in very simple, plain language, the reader will understand the reason for it.

This introduction to a discussion of the mind is, I feel, necessary because most of us have closed minds. It is an example of having to condition the reader's mind for what follows. So many of us are so set and so stereotyped in our outlook that unless ideas presented to us come in an acceptable pattern we reject them. In exactly the same way we tend to ignore, reject, or react badly to people who do not please us.

Many of the familiar, commonplace phrases we use so freely are proof of this. For example, we say, "You sure are a headache!" This statement declares that the other person poses a problem to me. The presence of a problem immediately implies undue pressure and anxiety. In an attempt to cope with the stress I concentrate on resolving it or struggle to shake free from it and end up with a splitting headache.

Or let us consider another common phrase. "He really is a pain in the neck." The word *pain*, like the word *ache*, is indicative of suffering. Real, genuine, intense discomfort is meant. Why in the neck? Because the neck, like the brain, is the seat of the nerve system that affects the entire person when mental stress is experienced.

These are simply two ordinary examples of how our mental attitudes and reactions towards stress can cause crippling effects in the physical body. I bring them out at the very beginning simply to show how intimately intertwined are body and mind.

The major difficulty with most of us is that we do not recognize that our minds are really divided into two areas of activity. There is the conscious or surface level which we are more or less aware of at all times. With training, discipline, and experience we can learn to control this area of our thinking. We can maintain acceptable attitudes most of the time. We can condition ourselves to behave properly under most conditions, even under provocation or tension. We can more or less convince others we are masters of ourselves.

But down at a much deeper level, if we are honest with ourselves, we discover that the realm of the subconscious is much less well controlled. Where on the surface we may show a brave and even beautiful front to the world, down below may lie a whole host of fears and formidable fantasies.

It is these unexpressed thoughts, impulses, and varied imaginations which can wreak havoc with our health. This really is where the root of so much ill health lies. We may not even be aware that fears, anxieties, worry, and tension are nourished by the deep, innermost attitudes of the subconscious mind. But they are. Just recognizing that this is so will oftentimes help to mend the condition.

Most of us tend to try to suppress thoughts, ideas, impulses, or imaginations which we feel are offensive. Too often we simply push them down into our subconscious minds. There they tend to ferment. Occasionally a bubble or two of their noxious products will force through to the surface of our conscious mind, surprising us with their virulence and vehemence. We may even wonder where such a weird or terrible thought could come from. Yet all the time subconsciously we may be fermenting the most atrocious ideas.

This principle applies especially to fretting and worrying about the future. Apart from a few confirmed "worrywarts" who seem to find a perverted pleasure in worrying, most people do not want to worry. Their conscious minds reject and repudiate the thought of "borrowing sorrow from tomorrow." They tend to suppress anxiety and instead of facing it for what it is, push it down, out of sight, so to speak, into their subconscious minds.

There in the dark recesses at the back of their mind the fret goes on fermenting. The tension has not been released. It has only been relocated. So the subconscious keeps wrestling with it, worrying about it, building up stress and strain.

How can one cope with this condition? How is this sort of tension to be tamed? Can one really tackle the tyranny of so deep-seated a tyrant?

The answer is yes!

It has taken many years to discover a few simple steps to ease this sort of anxiety.

Perhaps the first and most important is one which the young seldom, if ever, discover, but which is one of the great benefits of advancing years. Namely, the straightforward fact that roughly 80 percent of our fears never materialize. About four out of five of our worst worries never mature. They are but imaginations in the dark depths of our mind which seem real enough in anticipation but do not actually occur.

This figure of 80 percent is not just guesswork. It has been arrived at through extensive research. And those of us who have lived long enough to look back on a good span of life know it to be true. There are so many extenuating, changing, unpredictable, and unknown circumstances at play in life that in many cases, by the time a crisis has been reached it is no longer a crisis. Circumstances change; people change; other events enter the scene; and we ourselves alter our minds so much that often what looms as a calamity in due course levels out to be but a minor matter. What we imagined was an unclimbable mountain is stepped over like a small molehill.

It takes a certain amount of common sense and hard-headed reality to convince ourselves of this sometimes. But doing so will immediately dispel a great many of the dark, depressing anxieties that might otherwise haunt us.

A second helpful step to easing tension of this sort is simply not to borrow sorrow. The Scriptures teach us clearly that each day has sufficient of its own trouble without mort-gaging tomorrow.

There is a certain sublime sort of serenity which can settle in over the person who learns to live in "day-tight" compart-ments. This sounds simple to say. It takes a lifetime of living to learn. Yesterday is gone forever. It cannot be relived or repeated. The decisions that were made, the things that were done, the words that were spoken cannot be undone. There is no point in self-recrimination or self-abuse for any mistakes made. It will not undo the damage or erase the words. What has been, has been, and it must be left at that. Do not drag the dregs from yesterday into today. It does no good. It only fouls up the bright prospects of this day.

As for tomorrow, neither you nor I nor anyone else has any guarantee whatever that we shall be here. No one can say for certain that he will see the dawn of another day. And even if he does, he knows not what that day holds. Anything can happen.

The net result, then, is that we really have only *today*. Yes-terday is gone, tomorrow is unknown. Only these few hours in our hands now can we be sure of at all. As such they are exceedingly precious—precious because they are passing, precious because they are nonrepeatable, precious because in them we should live as though they were the only ones we have.

As we learn to look at life this way we will discover that

we can hardly afford to waste the present moment on worry. What is more, we find tremendous release in living for this day, not for tomorrow. We find a certain inner focusing of all our strength upon making the most of today. This gives sudden new awareness of our world in the immediate *Now*.

No longer do our minds drift off into endless dreams and imaginations and worries about tomorrow, next week, or the months to come. What is more, because this day is so precious all that is done and said during it takes on special meaning, special significance. Now we live in depth—depths that include even our subconscious mind. Living at these levels we find a certain cleansing, refreshing stream of thought surging through us to flush away all the fears and forebodings which may have fermented there before.

The third secret for taming the tensions which are rooted deep in our subconscious minds is that of simple living. One of the great seers has said, "The secret to life is simplify, simplify." This theme has already been stressed in this book. Most of us tend to bite off much more than we can chew in life. And because we cannot chew what we have bitten off we tend to take life in lumps and have difficulty digesting it at all.

Too many of us take on too much. We are overly ambitious, overly acquisitive, overly possessive. We are much better off to take just a little of anything at a time, taste it fully, and suck all the sweetness from it. "Enough is a feast."

We want so much, so fast, so soon. We are so intent on the thing or things we want we cannot enjoy the "getting." We so worry and fret about what we might acquire that we completely miss the pleasure of actually procuring it. When we can begin to concentrate upon the common activities, work, thought, or means of getting what we want, then suddenly our subconscious thoughts are switched from worrying about the end to enjoying the actual *means* that lead to the end. This gives us immediate release from tension, enabling us to appreciate the simple little delights of enjoying the immediate moment as we work towards our goal.

This is a rather difficult self-discipline to describe. Perhaps as an author I can best illustrate it by telling how I write a book. If I think only of a completed book in its entirety the task seems so tremendous, the time so lengthy, the details so innumerable that it looms as an overwhelming burden to bear. So many have said to me, "Write a book? How could I? Never!! Such a terrific task."

But when I sit down to do a book, I see it not in completed form only, though that is the ultimate goal in mind. Instead I see each blank page coming as a new opportunity to put on paper something useful, something of value, something enduring. Sentence by sentence the whole structure is steadily constructed. Each page is a new challenge, a new focus for thought. In this there is joy. And before I know it the task is done, the book complete.

We cannot live life in lumps. That produces indigestion. Live it a little at a time. Enjoy it as you savor it. This relieves the tension and adds zest to living.

Many of the emotional upheavals which plague people arise from anxiety over getting things done in time. We are apprehensive of deadlines. They are like swords suspended above our heads. They exert enormous pressure upon us. Time itself becomes a fearsome tyrant that enslaves us with the thought that we simply must meet certain critical claims upon us. The sense of being behind virtually drives some to distraction.

The way to tame this tension is simply not to take on more than one can comfortably handle. Basically what this boils down to in many instances is simply being brave enough to say no when asked to assume more assignments than we can handle. Incidentally this saying no applies not only to others, but to ourselves as well. Far too often we knowingly tackle jobs or undertake tasks which we are fully aware will wear us out in trying to get them done by certain deadlines.

A peculiar aspect to the matter of biting off more than one can chew is the way its insidious tension actually reduces efficiency. There is a common tendency to become unstrung, nervous, excited, and a bit flabbergasted when faced with more than can be handled. Much useful strength and energy are dissipated just in fretting over the matter. Some people will take a stab at this, then that, jumping erratically from one task to another. There are much wasted motion and strength. The jobs are only half done and a sense of desperation hangs over them. Undue tension is generated and one can soon break down under its inexorable tyranny.

Learning to say no is not an easy art. Most of us like to be called upon to help. We feel wanted and needed. It does something for our ego to think we are asked to do this or that. But it can also put us under undue pressure. With the passing years we must learn just how much we can handle comfortably and efficiently. Then, not only will the jobs be done better, but we ourselves will be freed from anxiety and will be able to enjoy greater serenity of mind and emotions.

Perhaps my favorite Chinese proverb states simply, "He who travels gently, travels far." It is well worth noting. When we come to appreciate fully the implication of living in day-tight compartments, we will discover the need to live through the day gently. We simply cannot live under terrible pressures, crowding and spurring ourselves to undue exertions, if we expect to live long, useful lives.

Of course it can be argued that it is better to live briefly and intensely rather than long and languidly. I am not advocating indolence or laziness when I say it is wise to live gently. It is possible to achieve a very great deal and still be gentle about it, both with ourselves and others.

This is not the sort of thing I could have or would have written twenty-five years ago. I am by nature a relentless "driver." I drove myself hard and I drove others around me hard. I lived under terrific tension and my tremendous drive created great tensions in those I worked and lived with. By the time I was thirty-five I had attained practically every ambition I ever set for myself. But I was a broken man, well-nigh washed up on the scrap heap of total collapse.

Sometimes this has to happen to us before we slow down, come to a stop, and take a long hard look at ourselves. Undue introspection is not a healthy exercise. But occasionally it is wise to pull off to the side of the road, so to speak, and take a little time to find out exactly where we are going and how fast.

Most of us, if we are honest with ourselves, will admit that we live too fast, too erratically, too crudely, and too thoughtlessly. The remedy or antidote for all of this is to live gently.

It takes time to be a gentleman or a gentlewoman. It takes time to be pleasingly polite. It takes time to perform the little courtesies that count for so much happiness in life. It takes time to enjoy each day with its little delights. It is this sort of gentle living that tames tension. Gentle living suddenly makes the mundane world seem really quite wonderful. It is what makes life's road quite a pleasant path instead of a torturous trail.

For some of us, learning to live this way is not easy. It demands self-discipline, concentration, and earnest endeavor. But it is surely well worthwhile. Occasionally, when we come to the end of a day during which we *know* we have lived gently and graciously, a warm aura of serene well-being engulfs us. Somehow it seems so good just to have been alive.

Almost everyone can remember such interludes in his life. They are like quiet, calm, glowing spring days after the stormy, blustery weather of a long, wild winter. Relaxation, warmth, and pleasure replace the stern tension of stressful weather.

9

Disciplined Thinking

Very few writers would devote an entire chapter to the subject of disciplined thinking, especially in a period of human history when permissiveness is the password. Be that as it may, this is something which we must examine and examine very carefully.

It is just as true to say, "We are what we think," as it is to say, "We are what we eat." It will be noted that *I did not say*, "We are what we think we are." This latter, unfortunately, is the delusion under which so many people live. They imagine themselves to be all sorts of things which they never really are. They visualize themselves in quite glowing colors while the real life portrait may be quite paltry. They create in their own minds an alluring concept of themselves which may be quite unlike their own true self.

In the realm of the mind and emotions, "we are what we think." That is to say, those subjects and matters and people which dominate our minds most of the time determine what sort of people we will be. The Scriptures state very clearly, "As a man thinketh in his heart, so is he" (Prov. 23:7).

This, then, being the case, it must follow as a very natural corollary that what I choose to think about is extremely important, first because it determines what kind of person I become, and second because it decides how my days shall be spent.

It is surprising how few people have ever really thought this through. Actually most people give much more consideration to what they eat than to what they think. There are millions of very sincere men and women who pay meticulous attention to their bodily diet yet never spend five minutes on their mental diet. They will exercise the greatest discretion in their choice of food but rarely give a passing thought to what their minds are fed. They will spend considerable sums of money and go to much trouble to procure the finest fare to eat but spend not a dollar for or devote an hour to nourishing their minds.

It seems absurd when one stops to think about it. Still it is all too true. If as much care were given to what we think about as is given to what we eat, half our mental ills would be remedied almost overnight. What is even more important, many emotional difficulties would never develop.

The rather amazing and cheering aspect of this otherwise pathetic picture is that we all have it within our own power to choose what we will think about. This is a very personal and very private area of life in which we are, for the most part, perfectly free to think about whatever we wish.

The trouble is that most of us have never been taught or trained to choose deliberately what we will think. We drift along from day to day woolgathering or daydreaming about the most innocuous subjects. The rigid disciplining of the mind is a practice known to very few. Yet those who undertake this practice can in large measure become masters of themselves. They need no longer be subject to every passing whim or fancy that can create tension or turmoil in their thinking.

Let me give a simple illustration of the sort of tyranny to which many minds are subjected. Take the matter of an ordinary letter which a girl may expect to receive from her steady boyfriend. When it does not arrive her mind begins to race. She imagines all sorts of things that could have happened. Perhaps he was in an accident. Maybe he is losing interest in her. Could it be he has found a more attractive lady friend? And so her mind, now completely out of control, leaps wildly from one fantasy to another. Terrible tension and excruciating anxiety build up. The stress intensifies and she is tortured with all sorts of fears, misgivings, and evil foreboding.

A day or two later the boyfriend shows up. She finds him as friendly and affectionate as ever. The fact is he did write and gave the letter to a friend who offered to drop it into a mailbox. But the friend forgot, and the letter is still stuck in his pocket.

A person with a disciplined mind would have taken a much different approach to this dilemma. When the letter did not arrive, such a person would decide quietly and calmly that several simple, ordinary things might have happened. Her boyfriend might have been busy or called away on another job so there was no time to write. Or if he wrote he might simply have forgotten to mail the letter. It could even have gone astray in the post office. But because she knows him well, she can count on him. She trusts his integrity. She is sure things will work out well. This is disciplined thinking. It is positive, not negative. It concentrates on the good, not the bad.

The entire subject of learning to think positive, good, and noble thoughts is one of the greatest secrets to mental serenity. Our minds, like other parts of our makeup, prefer to follow certain fixed patterns of behavior. We are notorious creatures of habit. Once we begin to behave in a certain manner it seems ever so hard to "switch tracks," so to speak.

But learning to switch tracks is the sure path to taming tension. It is the trick that can turn us from being worn-down worrywarts to buoyant, brave individuals with a beautiful outlook on life.

Again and again we hear it said, "Oh, he has a one-track mind." And it is indeed true of many people. Instead of being masters of their own minds and disciplining them to think about a variety of wholesome, worthwhile subjects, they simply allow their minds to lead them down the same old tiresome track of trouble and worry.

Perhaps I can best illustrate what I mean by using a rather simple illustration from everyday life. By nature I am one who enjoys variety in life If, therefore, I set out to travel to a remote spot which I have visited many times before, I always try, if possible, to find a new and different way to go. I will take special pains to choose a route that offers a fresh view of the countryside and adds pleasure to traveling by taking me into new territory. If perchance I traveled a rough country road full of ruts and potholes before, then I am doubly delighted to find a better, smoother road. I am not at all keen to plow my way through the same old ruts and mudholes every time. I have been that way before. I have been bogged down too often to want a repeat performance. There is nothing very heroic about going into a situation where I am sure to hit bottom again.

Precisely the same applies to our thought life and thinking behavior. Again and again we allow ourselves to travel down the same old rutted road of muddy thinking that we have been over a hundred times before. Simply for lack of determination we wallow through the same old worries and stumble over the same old troubles. We torture ourselves with the stress and strain of struggling through the sloughs and swamps of depression and despondency in which we were bogged before.

Most of us simply submit to the tyranny of our thoughts, shrug our shoulders in despair, and say, "I just can't help it." This is delusion. We can change all this if we want to. The question is, "Do we want to?"

If so, what is required is a bit of dogged determination. We must make a positive decision to switch our thinking, to change the route we will take, to set our minds on other matters, to become masters of our own thoughts and where they will travel.

It is utterly appalling how many people are helpless victims of their own imaginations. It is their own ideas and their own thoughts which literally lead them around by the nose both day and night. All the old problems of fear, misapprehension, suspicion, falsehoods, tension, misunderstanding, and stress attend their travel through life.

Now life was never intended to be that way. Our thought life was never meant to be a torturous route of strain and anxiety. Rather, we were given free wills with which to choose intelligently what sort of path our thoughts would follow.

I say this in absolute earnestness. I affirm that it is perfectly possible for a person to step out of the old ruts of self-pity, worry, and anxiety onto the high road of lofty living and hope. But to do it one must switch tracks. One has to have something fine, noble, beautiful, and inspiring upon which to center one's attention and place one's mind. If there is to be an alternative route to take, some time, thought, and concentration are required to find it.

Exactly at this point is where most people fail. They will not discipline themselves to think about other things. The Scriptures are very explicit about this. We read, "Whatsoever things are true, whatsoever things are honest, whatsoever things are just, whatsoever things are pure, whatsoever things are lovely, whatsoever things are of good report; if there be any virtue, and if there be any praise, *think on these things!*" (Phil. 4:8).

There is, of course, one catch to all of this. If one has not been in the habit of thinking about other things, where does one begin? If the mind is a mess, filled with nothing but negative and destructive thoughts, how can one help but fall back into the same old rut?

It is here that some of the hints given in the first part of this book are like steppingstones to help us control our minds.

First, if we want to change some of the scenery on the walls of our minds, so to speak, we simply have to get outside the four familiar walls of our homes. It is astonishing how the patterns of our thoughts are in large measure conditioned by the sameness of our surroundings.

So it is a tremendous impetus to taking ourselves in hand if we will simply take the positive step of going out the door, shutting it behind us, and enjoying a stroll in the fresh air and sunshine. In exactly the same way we should close the door of our minds to all the old familiar thoughts, leave them behind, and deliberately open ourselves to all the new and fresh impulses coming to us from the world around.

Perhaps for the first time in months we may actually see a rosebud opening to the sun. Stop and touch its velvet petals with the tips of your fingers. Have you felt anything that smooth or delicate for weeks? Bend down and inhale its fragrance. Not once or twice, but long and deeply. What pleasant memories occur as you relish its rich aroma? Perhaps its perfume reminds you of a beautiful and gracious girl or woman you admire. Look into the heart of the rose. Note the tints of changing colors in its throat. See how smoothly each separate petal is folded upon its mate. Whence this delicate design, this magnificent and mysterious unfolding to the sun?

All this may take less than ten minutes' time but it has perhaps transported you a thousand miles away from your old self-centeredness to places and people that lift your spirits and refresh your hopes. You see, so many of the very satisfying, very fine, very noble impulses in life are all around us. All that is required is the time to expose ourselves to their inspiration and uplift. Too many of us think that only an appointment with a psychologist or a psychiatrist can cure our condition. Much more often the remedy is readily at hand in the natural world around us.

Take a simple thing like a bird's song. When was the last time you really listened to a bird sing? When did you actually stop whatever you were doing and step outside to hear a tiny songster sing his heart out in the hedge? Has it occurred to you that this is done with total abandon and utter freedom? He sings simply with great goodwill. Perhaps he is one of a species that has flown several thousand miles to reach your backyard. Have you ever imagined the stamina required for so small a body to travel so far over mountains, plains, lakes, and rivers to reach this precise point? If you have, you are beginning to learn to switch tracks in your thought life. It is quite impossible for any person to expose himself long and often to nature without an ennobling effect. It is one of the surest routes one can take to find tranquility of mind instead of stress and tension.

When it comes to people the problem is somewhat more complex. There is no doubt whatever that most wrong thinking has as its source misunderstanding between human beings.

Added to this is the curse of human conversation. The word *curse* is used advisedly and with great care. There is no better description of our human tendency to talk about each other. Some of the things said and thought may be complimentary. Far more often they are not. Far too many of our thoughts about one another are far from flattering or complimentary.

Because of this the general caliber of conversation in any community of human beings is at a rather low level. If we do not actually malign others, many of us do, at least, tend to deprecate them a bit. Gossip, it seems, is the favorite pastime of human beings, and the damage it does is incalculable. Worse still, once we have indulged ourselves in this malicious habit, it hangs over our heads with a deep sense of guilt. We know we can be held accountable for our wretched remarks. It puts us under tension and we are caught in the snare of our own making.

There is only one way to avoid taking this torturous trail through life. That is, find another path. Think other thoughts. Concentrate your conversation on other subjects. Spend your mental energies on greater and more noble matters than mere gossip.

A cardinal rule which my first wife always taught our children was, "If you can't say anything kind about other people, don't say anything!" This is an excellent piece of counsel, but it is only half the solution. One has to get beyond this and actually switch his thoughts to things or people so fine and noble that it is easy and natural to speak well of them. Let us look for the good in others and dwell on it. Let us make much of their merits and forget their faults.

It has been well said that all of us have something of the

divine and something of the devil in our makeup. Each of us has something of the saint and something of the sinner. So if we would release ourselves from the tension of guilt that assails those who talk about others in a derogatory way, we will have to learn the kindly art of thinking only good things about them. It is so very easy to fall into the habit of criticizing and censuring others. It requires intelligent self-discipline to think the best of other human beings.

The person who masters this attitude finds himself traveling on a highway of happiness. There is a lighthearted gaiety to his living. Gone is the guilt over grinding someone else into the ground. In its place are a bright smile and a contented mind at peace with other people. Instead of pulling them apart we praise their good points. We find that our faith in their better qualities tends to inspire their spirits. This is a case of switching tracks. What a thrilling adventure, free from fret, life can be when we choose to think this way.

Perhaps it would be useful at this point to discuss the matter of humor. Some of us cannot always see something fine or noble in a situation. But very often we can see something humorous. Even this is a step in the right direction. And doubly so, if we can learn to laugh at ourselves. It is a tremendous tonic both for ourselves and those around us if we learn to laugh easily and not take life too seriously.

Even more important, a rich sense of humor provides enormous release from the tyranny of most tensions. The moment we see humor either in a situation or in people, the fear and foreboding vanish. Most of us take ourselves and life in general too seriously. This does not mean that we should not have very deep convictions and be utterly sincere in the way we behave. But a sense of humor is essential to a balanced and wholesome outlook on life.

Some leading psychologists go so far as to assert that humor can be one's best friend in maintaining a healthy, well-disciplined mind. And certainly it is common knowledge that gaiety and lighthearted humor contribute enormously to good health and general well-being. One should deliberately look for the funny side of life—not at others' expense but out of unbounded good nature. It's there if you look for it.

I do not refer to the snide, sarcastic humor which is becoming increasingly popular. Nor to the smutty jokes with double meanings or the smart sophistication of the intellectual dilettante. Rather I refer to that hilarious humor which can come so suddenly into any situation to give us hearty laughs that can relax both ourselves and all others around us.

I have always held enormous respect and admiration for people with a keen sense of humor. In fact they draw me like a magnet. I love to be in their company. The fun and gaiety that enfold them are like a lovely warm glow in which I can readily relax. I come away feeling refreshed, cleansed, and set free from the fret and strain of life.

Finally, in dealing with the subject of a disciplined mind, making decisions should be discussed. Just making up our minds can be one of the most trying experiences during the day. In fact we may keep putting it off again and again so that the decision drags on over days, weeks, sometimes months, and in extreme cases even years. This indecision is one of the most destructive and damaging forces that can exert enormous pressure upon us. As one dear old man said to me once, "Life would be all fun if it wasn't for the decisions."

The story is told of a mule tied up between two bales of hay. Because he couldn't make up his mind which to eat first, he kept turning from one to the other. Finally he fell dead with exhaustion and hunger between the two bales; he hadn't touched either one.

Again the secret is, one must discipline oneself to *do* something. One must act. And perhaps the simplest formula for helping fretful folk is to take a piece of blank paper and draw a line down the middle. On each side write down in simple sentences the reasons *for* and *against* taking a certain course of action.

Depending on the relative importance of each reason, give it one, two, or three points of merit. When all the reasons have been written down and their total merits added up arithmetically, the decision will be evident. It is surprising how well this works. It is also quite astonishing how greatly the reasons on one side generally outweigh those on the other.

Another helpful practice, especially for people who are inclined to be scatterbrains, is to *make a list* of all the tasks they want to do during the day. These should then be arranged in a simple consecutive order so that one is not rushing around with wasted motion and wasted time.

It is generally a good idea, if possible, to put the most disagreeable and difficult task first. Once you have done this, half the battle is won. You have really decided to do the job and do it first. Actually this is a perfect example of doing the thing we fear. Most of us cringe from making decisions and doing things lest we make a wrong choice and carry out the wrong plan. But we cannot live like this. I used to tell my own youngsters as they were growing up, "The person who has never done anything wrong has never done anything!"

All of us are bound by our very fallible human nature to make some errors in judgment and some mistaken moves. It is simply part of living. When we face this fact, half the fear of doing the wrong thing disappears. Suddenly we are much more serene and the making of a decision becomes less demanding. Instead of cringing from the choice we now rise to accept a challenge.

It is possible, by implementing the few very simple suggestions above, to go through the average day with little or no distress over our decisions. We simply discipline ourselves to put things in their proper priority; we do not take on more than we can handle; we decide important issues on paper; then we proceed without fear to do what we would otherwise put off.

To live this way is to live with great loads lifted from the mind. It sets us free to enjoy the day and revel fully in every delight it brings us.

10

Improving the Mind

"Improving the mind" is an old-fashioned expression that has passed out of use. This does not mean it is any less important than it used to be. Quite the contrary. In our highly complex society it becomes an absolute imperative.

Because of extensive exposure to the mass media, it is generally assumed that this generation is much better informed than was its forebears. This statement cannot be disputed if we are thinking only in terms of mere technical information. But that really is not what this chapter is about.

The theme of this book is not technology, but taming tension. And one of the main reasons it has been written is that minds now more than ever before break down under the stress of modern living. Modern man seems, in spite of all his superior technology, incapable of coping with the tensions generated in the twentieth century. Approximately one out of every six people becomes mentally ill to the point where he requires professional help. Government social agencies are taxed to the limit in caring for people with troubled minds. Much of the social work and personal counseling done by churches and other benevolent agencies centers in helping men and women with warped minds.

Far too often all these well-meaning endeavors deal only with the symptoms of the mentally sick, rather than with the root of their problem. They are more preoccupied with cures than causes.

The mind, like the body, is an organism which, if it is to grow, mature, and flourish must be nourished. The vast majority of human beings pay very careful attention to eating. At least they do make sure some fresh food is consumed every day. Yet remarkably few people, once they are out of school, do much to nourish their minds.

As a matter of fact, it is true to say that most minds are actually starved. Little wonder that so many are stunted. They are quite incapable of coping with the pressures and responsibilities placed upon them.

Now it is probably not well known that in part the ability of our minds to function efficiently does depend on the actual physical food we eat. Thinking represents the expenditure of energy just as surely as does manual labor or athletic activity. And all over the world we have incredible illustrations of impoverished people with equally impoverished minds. Likewise we have learned that much of the lethargy and lack of initiative in some races can be attributed directly to a deficient diet. So to feel and think well, one must eat well and intelligently.

Anyone, for example, who believes he can do heavy mental work or intense study, week after week, on a meager diet of coffee, cigarettes, and inferior carbohydrate meals is headed for a collapse. The body and the brain and the mind are all tightly interwoven into one complex mechanism. The man who is so shortsighted as to deny himself a properly balanced diet, high in protein, minerals, and vitamins, is bound to subsist at a fairly low intellectual level.

There is no need to elaborate further on this point here. It follows, naturally, that if one eats well, one will feel energetic and alert. The mind will be active and it will be open and eager to receive new ideas and fresh impulses. The question is: Do we supply it with sufficient mental nourishment? Do we actually make it our business to see that it is supplied with fresh food for thought?

Actually most of us are mentally lazy. We do not want to discipline our minds for sustained thinking. We do not wish to develop elasticity and muscle in our thinking. We prefer to drift through life in a dreamy sort of way, seldom doing anything very positive to actually improve our minds.

The net result is that when we are brought under pressure or exposed to problems that arouse anxieties we cannot rise to their challenge. With little or no resilience to resist the trouble, we tend to give way and break down. There are no mental resources available nor instinctive intelligence with which to tackle our tensions and tame their tyranny.

The mental behavior of many adults is really very immature. It can be said to resemble that of a child. Men and women well on in years often respond and react to adverse circumstances not like adults, but like adolescents. They have never matured in their thinking. They have done nothing to improve their minds. Their attitudes are juvenile and irresponsible. Rather than face life they flee from it. Under adversity they become totally demoralized, sinking into deep despair.

There are ways and means to meet these difficulties. The simple, unvarnished truth is that all of us are bound to have troubles. There is no such thing as a life without some trouble. The question is: How can or do I take it? Can I develop mental resources with which to meet the pressures put upon me?

The answer is a simple yes!

The mind, like the body, is conditioned by what it consumes. If our mental fare is unfit for us we will have weak and impoverished minds. If we make it our business to take in only the best, we can be sure of robust and vigorous mental health.

Again it is a matter of our wills. It is a question of deciding what we will do with our time. It is a case of choosing constructive material that will build us up or damaging material that can destroy us. We are not mere pawns pushed about on the chessboard of life by a relentless fate. We can become to a large degree what we want to be. But this takes a certain amount of self-discipline and solid determination.

What goes into our minds in large measure determines what will come out of them when called upon to meet any emergency. How they have been conditioned by careful study and habitual practice will decide how we cope with the complexities of life. How we equip and furnish our minds from day to day will determine whether or not we can stand the stresses and tame the tensions of twentieth-century society.

Probably the most obvious manner in which we can improve our minds is by choosing carefully what we will read. Reading is perhaps less universal than it once was because of competition from radio, TV, films, and other forms of mass media. Nevertheless, it is still true to say that the choice of good reading material is one of the surest ways to improve one's mind.

Because the array of books, magazines, newspapers, and scientific publications is so enormous people have real difficulty in deciding what is worth reading. The flood of inferior and sordid material spewed from printing presses all over the world makes it ever more challenging to sort out what is useful and helpful from that which is decidedly destructive. This should not discourage one from choosing choice books and magazines. One of the rewarding aspects of reading is that it can not only improve our minds, but also at the same time provide us with enormous pleasure, relaxation, and adventure. Too many people regard reading as a penance. It need not be. It can become one of the most joyous interludes in the day to which we look forward eagerly with keen anticipation.

The selection of suitable books will depend on the degree of one's own mental development. It will also be decided in part by one's personal interests. But above all the books should be of such a caliber that they inspire our lives, challenge our minds, and enlarge our awareness.

In this connection I would heartily recommend good biographies of some truly great men and women. Awareness of the noble achievements of other mortals gives us great hope for ourselves. We see them meeting the trials of their times to triumph over trouble, and are inspired to do likewise.

There is something decidedly thrilling and uplifting about biographies. I recall clearly how my earliest boyhood dreams, aspirations, and hopes were molded by men like Theodore Roosevelt, Cherry Kearton, Carl Akeley, and other great outdoorsmen who combined a love of wild places and wild things with a great passion to preserve them for posterity. I never met one of these men except through books. Yet in large measure they expanded the horizons of my mind and laid upon me a consuming concern for conservation which has colored my entire life.

But while the books performed this great service, they also provided me with enormous pleasure. Again and again during my troubled teen-age years when I was under terrible tensions just trying to get through school, I turned to these books for strength of mind and fortitude of will to carry on. They were a tremendous antidote to tensions which otherwise might have crushed me.

Another wondrous influence that good books of this kind have upon us is their impact on our subconscious minds. We begin to identify with our heroes and heroines. We picture ourselves succeeding as they succeeded. We visualize ourselves as victors. We set before ourselves the picture of one who has achieved. Subconsciously we strive and aim for that end. And in this we find enormous strength of mind and purpose of will.

Next to biographies, books on natural history, outdoor life, travel, and true-life adventures in exploration are to be recommended. All these subjects, if well written about, have the benefit of enlarging our knowledge of the world around us while taking us into far-reaching territory outside ourselves. They sharpen our awareness of the beauty and wonder to be found in the flowers, trees, rocks, birds, mountains, seas, and animals that share the planet with us. They also arouse an appetite for adventure and exploration on our own part.

The other reason I have recommended such books is that they do not burden us with the never-ending problems and complexities of our times. So much modern writing concerns itself almost exclusively with the dilemmas of human society. In part that is a product of the urban mind which is invariably preoccupied with the problems and pathos of humanity.

Though we recognize the important place occupied by man on the planet, we need not always give him first place in our thinking. To always absorb ourselves in the complexities of our society is to become somewhat skeptical and jaded. For balance of outlook and freshness of mind we must of necessity turn to the wondrous world around us. For it is indeed wondrous and thrilling and inspiring despite the very worst that men have done to it.

This applies especially to the reading of newspapers and magazines. Far too much of our time and attention is given to gulping down doses of bad news, scandal, and distress every day. For reasons which completely escape most of us, and in spite of all the excuses offered to explain it, we fail to understand why newspapers print bad news much more often than good news. There is the human tendency to pervert even the pleasant in life, but just why our minds and emotions should be strained and stressed almost every day with adverse news is a bit beyond most people.

This fact becomes even more formidable when we stop to realize that modern communication makes it possible to deposit all the world's troubles on our doorstep every day. It was never intended that we should have to stand such stress continuously. Consequently I make no apologies for urging you to forget the daily paper for a while. If you want to tame some of your tensions, stop taking the daily paper. Just one good dose a week of that deluge of trouble should be enough.

In place of the paper there are excellent journals available. Many of them present a much better and more balanced view of world affairs. At least they make us think for ourselves rather than predigesting material for us.

A recent and most helpful development in the realm of the printed word is the advent of the cheap paperback. The best of books can be procured this way for a minimum of expense. I have a number in my own private library. They are doubly precious because I can slip them in my pocket and enjoy them anywhere when I go outdoors to relax. Some of them have been reread several times, bringing fresh joy and tremendous exhilaration to the hours I spend in the sun or beside the sea. They are real tension tamers.

Pocket books or paperbacks with pornographic material are to be avoided. They are intended to arouse the reader, producing a variety of anxieties and stresses related to sex. It is a wise person who will deliberately avoid this fare for his mind.

Much the same can be said for fiction. It is not generally known that for fiction writing to be successful it must maintain throughout its pages what is referred to as "tension" or "the tension line." This is what attracts the reader's attention and holds the mind in suspense. The more tense the narrative, the greater the grip. It forces one to press on relentlessly page after page, wondering what will happen next and how the plot will finally be resolved.

Fiction of this sort may be fine for entertainment but it does little or nothing to develop or improve the mind. Outstanding historical novels, if well and thoroughly researched, may provide some insight into past events. Likewise pleasant romances may be somewhat of an escape for those who indulge in them. But their total benefit is meager and time can be much better spent in other types of reading.

Children and young people should be encouraged to read books of the very highest caliber. A steady diet of comics, thrillers, and crime stories is bound to produce anxiety problems at some point for those who persist in pursuing this material.

Finally there is the whole field of concentrated study. There are many men and women who, though they had few opportunities for schooling, have applied themselves diligently to serious study and become experts in various professions. Admittedly such individuals are exceptional. But for the great majority of us it is perfectly possible to find enormous mental benefit from taking up a special study of some field which interests us. When we do, we discover that we are embarking on a tremendous adventure which may well prove to be a mainstay all through life.

It matters not what the subject is. It can be almost anything from astronomy to architecture, from orchids to automobiles, from rabbits to modern art. The important thing is that it provide a center upon which one's reading interests can focus. It should catch us up in a cause that expands the mind and widens the horizons of our understanding.

In one sense this sort of reading and thinking almost becomes a hobby. Yet it is more than just a hobby for it entails disciplining the mind and applying the intellect to the subject at hand. There is pleasure in such a pursuit. It also helps to ease us over the trying tensions and petty irritations that attend the daily round of living. It is a splendid counteraction to the burdensome boredom that bears down on so many in modern metropolitan areas.

With such reading habits our minds may continue to grow and be ever quickened even though the routine of our everyday life seems stable and static.

11

Viewing Habits

It has been well said that "one look is worth a thousand words." Looking at something tends to absorb the total attention of the viewer more than does contact through any of the other senses. Certainly it commands our concentration much better than does hearing. It is, for example, perfectly easy to hear a radio in the background while we are busy about many other duties. Whereas if one's eyes are focused on something it is much more difficult to be distracted or give our attention to an alternative interest.

It is for this reason that TV is considered a much more effective medium of communication than is radio. Because it combines both viewing and hearing it is regarded as more impressive than reading alone.

These are debatable points simply because what reading does for one person it may not do for another. Similarly what TV means to many it certainly does not to others. TV actually repels some people. Its programming is so pathetic it borders on being an insult to the intelligence.

At one stage I determined to do a series of TV programs

with the Canadian Broadcasting Corporation. The aim was to produce something of special merit for the viewers. The net result was a response beyond my fondest hopes. Letters came in from all over the country commenting on the exceptional quality and high standard of the series, so much so that the programs were shown four times.

This demonstrates that people do appreciate something fine to look at. Subconsciously they hunger for that which will improve and enlarge their outlook. They want to watch something which is not inane. The strange thing is that even though this be so, still they will sit for hours and allow their vision to be filled with all sorts of crude characters and inferior material. Sensible people who would ordinarily despise anything degrading will permit all sorts of violence, crime, murders, shootings, perversion, and luridness to be performed in the privacy of their own homes on the TV screen.

This grip of the screen upon the mind and emotions of the viewer needs our careful consideration. Children and young people who are exposed continuously to the garbage that comes out of the minds of TV producers are being subjected to very real emotional and mental stresses.

It is well-nigh impossible for anyone, be he young or old, to spend hours each week witnessing crimes, violence, and perversion without being himself subjected to intense emotional tensions. These tensions may be dismissed from the conscious mind with a shrug and a laugh, saying, "Oh, well, it's just a show." But inevitably, deep down in the subconscious, damage has been done.

If we wish to spare ourselves the inevitable stress and strain which many TV programs produce, we simply have to exercise sufficient moral stamina to switch off the vulgar or violent material. Not only should we do this for our own sakes, but also for the benefit of our families.

Many older people find it hard to understand why those of the younger generation gravitate so readily to violence and perversion. The answer is simple. Any youngster exposed to these activities day after day is bound to be conditioned subconsciously to accept them as the normal thing to do. A juvenile who has seen a hundred robberies in his own living room might feel it would be fun to try the same tricks himself.

Such attitudes generate tremendous tensions between old and young. The generation gap between parents and their offspring is not a vacuum void of feeling. It is, rather, a gap charged with terrifying tensions and endless stress.

Some secrets to taming such tensions will be touched on in a subsequent chapter. Suffice it to say at this point that if parents wish to prevent the development of undue stress and strains in their homes they will monitor the TV carefully. Few aspects of twentieth-century living are so destructive of domestic tranquility as this one technological development.

Weak-willed people and those poorly informed look on TV as a great boon. It is to them a marvelous "baby sitter," a perfect "guest entertainer," an ideal "time killer," an "unfailing companion," and above all a "tremendous educator." The tragic truth is that in more cases than they realize it is the very thing which is tearing their lives down with its insidious stress.

It is not enough in a book of this sort to simply point out where a peril may lie. It is only right and proper that an antidote should be supplied. Already I have suggested that part of the secret to reducing this tension from television is simply to turn it off at times. Not all TV shows are stressful. Some are in fact both beneficial and beautiful. One simply must exercise self-discipline in deciding what shall be seen. This is plain common sense. Yet it is astonishing how few have the intellectual fortitude to flick off the switch.

But over and beyond this there must be an alternative. After all, during our waking hours, while our eyes are open, they must be fastened on something else if they are not on the screen. What will it be? The preceding chapter pointed out the enormous improvement of the mind that is possible through reading good books.

But if books which entail only reading are a bore, then what? I suggest profusely illustrated works. It is astounding how much pleasure and information one can derive from looking at pictures. Modern publications are becoming increasingly well illustrated. Often an hour or two spent leafing gently through a volume with beautiful photographs, prints, and color plates can be enormously rewarding. Not only are the pictures educational but they are delightfully relaxing. A great beauty to this sort of diversion is that one can turn to the same book again and again. Gradually it becomes like an old familiar friend whose pages afford one enormous enjoyment and genuine release from the tensions of the day.

To have beautiful books of this sort in the home does a lot, too, for the children. Of their own volition they will turn to them repeatedly to find the release and joy they subconsciously seek.

What has been said of books applies equally to the whole realm of pictures, painting, art, and photography.

It is quite remarkable how the pictures which we hang upon the walls of our home can influence our entire outlook on life. The home adorned with beautiful pictures of tranquil scenes is bound to be much more serene than one where there are few or none at all. It is even worse to decorate the home with garish, abstract art which has little meaning and often reflects only the tension and chaos of a sick society where stress and strain are so evident in every area of life.

The paintings and pictures recommended are those which can transport us from the pettiness of our immediate surroundings into a wider world beyond us. When I was a university student I was obliged to stay in a rather cramped and drab home one winter. Its rooms were small, its atmosphere bleak, and its owners very dull. The only truly redeeming feature about the place was a magnificent sunset scene that hung in the living room. Again and again I absorbed myself in its loveliness. It was a tremendous uplift and inspiration amid what otherwise would have been unbearable surroundings. I recall clearly, even yet, how that painting would bring a sense of peace and quietness and gentle contentment when all around my stern little world seemed harsh and hard.

Beautiful pictures need not be expensive. Magnificent prints are available at very low cost. They are one of the finest investments anyone can make for obtaining a more beautiful and balanced view of life. What is more, we do well to devote a little time each day to looking at them. It helps, too, to change the pictures around occasionally. Give some away and replace them with fresh scenes to inspire your outlook.

All the pictures in our homes need not be purchased. If one has the least penchant for drawing, sketching, or painting, this inclination should be pursued ardently. There are enormous pleasure, satisfaction, and fulfillment in doing one's own work.

I was well over forty years of age before I found sufficient courage to pick up pencil and pen to do my own drawings and ink sketches. At first the attempts were feeble and faltering. But by degrees the caliber of work improved. Eventually some of my sketches were used to illustrate my own books. Then I went beyond that and shared with friends a special few as Christmas cards. It astonished me to go into their homes and find my efforts adorning their walls and shelves, put there because of the joy and beauty they had brought into their homes.

There is something supremely rewarding about doing one's own work this way. It is a tremendous tonic for tension, besides being an outlet for creative instincts.

If one is earnest in one's efforts to draw or paint, one soon discovers that his entire attention is caught up in the task. It may seem a strange thing to say, but for many people this is the first time in life that they really begin to look at things. Suddenly light and shadow on stone, a leaf, or a building take on special significance. The shape of a cloud, the sparkle of the sea, the details of a fence, or the form of a flower acquire great interest. It is as if suddenly a misty veil has been drawn back from across one's vision. Instead of a blur the world is now seen as alive and vibrant. Each part of it pulses with light and color and a new fascination.

This new ability to really see, to sense the changing moods of the moment, to be open and receptive to the subtle interplay of the shifting scenes around one, is a wondrous thing. The marvel of this approach, this view of things, is that it transfers our attention from ourselves, our worries, and our anxieties to the tangible world around us. If we extend our interest even further by attempting to transfer to paper what our eyes behold, then we find ourselves totally absorbed.

Winston Churchill did not commence to do oil painting until he was well past forty. In writing about it later he made the remark that no man could really paint and worry at the same time. Art was for him a total release from the tensions of life. Even during the most difficult war years when this man carried such colossal responsibilities day and night, he turned to his paintbrushes and easel to find ease of mind and freshness of outlook.

What many people do not realize is that to draw well or paint effectively the artist must look hard and intently at his object. It is this intense concentration on the scene which helps us to view it in a deeper and more meaningful dimension. It heightens our awareness. It brings all our faculties of observation and memory into play. It makes us much more alive. All this adds to the quality and character of our work. But best of all this intense concentration becomes a most beneficial viewing habit for all of life, not just our art.

I recall very vividly being invited to go for a drive with a man who was in deep distress. His life had lost its zest. The world seemed a flat, stale, dull place to live. He was under stress and tension, worrying about his future and his family.

We were living on the prairies at the time. As we two men drove out across the somewhat monotonous plains my friend poured out his cup of complaint. Suddenly we came over a small rise of ground where a huge sweep of open country stretched to the horizon. In the wide skies giant cumulus clouds climbed toward heaven like huge white castles.

The scene gripped me. "Pull off to the side, Dean," I remarked. "Let's fill our minds with the majesty of this scene!" A bit bewildered and somewhat sheepish, Dean drove into the grass on the shoulder of the road and switched off the motor.

Quietly and gently I began to comment about the beautiful sky, about the magnificent cumulus formations, about the broad horizons, about the wild, free sweep of country. Almost at once I could sense a subtle yet profound change coming over my companion. The old anxieties and tensions were gradually being replaced by a flood of fresh appreciation for the wonder of the world around him.

After a few minutes he turned to me and said softly, "Phillip, I have lived on these prairies for years and years and I have never really noticed the beauty of the sky before. For the first time, this morning, I realize what I've been missing. I just didn't see it like this."

This may seem an incredible story. But it is true of thousands and thousands of people. Depending on how we view the world around us, there can be drabness or delight; there can be tiredness and tension or exciting aliveness and relaxation.

If drawing or painting is not a natural inclination, then try photography. It requires no great artistic talent to take excellent photographs. It does not even require an expensive camera. Some of the finest pictures have been taken by amateurs using cameras that cost less than thirty dollars.

Of course some people have a natural feeling for taking pictures. Their sense of balance and gift for composition are of a high caliber. Consequently it is not difficult for them to come up with very satisfying results.

But for those who are not so inclined there is still the thrill of improving one's techniques. Get some good books on basic composition. Study the photographs which do impress you; discover for yourself what it is that makes them outstanding; learn how to photograph very ordinary subjects in such a way as to make them unusually attractive.

All of this is an art in itself. It demands some thought. It takes time. It requires attention to details which in themselves are new discoveries. It heightens your awareness of beauty all about you. It brings new interest and enthusiasm into your life at almost every turn.

My wife is a keen amateur photographer. Again and again she surprises and delights me with the fresh approaches she brings to picture taking. Some of her ideas are departures from the ordinary and lead us both into brand new endeavors.

The net result is that the time and thought she has given to the subject reward us with outstanding pictures.

Her own photo album is a never-ending source of pleasure and relaxation to her. I often tease her about it, remarking that it is indeed a very good thing that photographs cannot be worn out by repeatedly looking at them. For her money I know of nothing which gives her one-tenth the pleasant relaxation which her photography does.

Another benefit is, of course, that this interest helps to take people outdoors. It gets them outside their four small walls. It expands their horizons. It gives them a whole new world that can be viewed while they are in it, and again and again in retrospect later on.

An evening spent in looking at beautiful slides can be an enormous pleasure for the photographer, his family, and his friends. In our own home my children would coax again and again to see the slides I had taken of wildlife and natural scenery in many countries. It was an interlude of relaxation for all of us. And for me in particular it meant reliving some of the most exciting episodes of my whole life.

Now it can be argued that one has neither the talent, time, money, nor inclination for any of the pursuits mentioned, be they books, paintings, art, or photography. This may be so. Still it is surprising that, if and when one really wants to do a thing, ways and means can always be found.

Nonetheless to all such may I say that our view of life can still be enhanced by such simple and ordinary steps as having a bowl of fruit on the living-room table. Even a cluster of wildflowers plucked from beside the path can bring a touch of newness to a room. The branch of a pine, bare twigs with their spring buds ready to burst, a few shells from the beach, a handful of stones from a stream, even the fallen feather of a wild bird will do something to enlarge our vision and take our minds into quiet meadows of thought.

Life for many is crowded with stress and strain. Yet much of its weariness can be counteracted with a cheerful outlook. To cultivate that outlook one must learn to look for the loveliness in the world around him.

For those who live in great cities and crowded metropolitan areas it is not always easy to find open spaces, wide skies, or forested areas. Perhaps deep inside, their hearts hunger for such release and their eyes ache for some fresh view on which to feast themselves. Such people should seek the semi-seclusion of a garden; even a tiny corner of a park or children's playground can provide release from always staring at crowded streets and concrete walls. Learn to look up, too, filling your vision with vistas of sky and clouds and the beauty of tree branches above the street.

Then, too, cities generally do have one compensation which helps to make up for the lack of picturesque country scenes. There one can find art galleries and art shops where an endless array of new pictures and new paintings pass on parade. In one city where I lived most of the proprietors of the art shops in town got to know me because of my frequent visits to enjoy the pictures. That I seldom made a purchase did not trouble them at all. They quickly learned how precious were the few moments I paused to refresh myself before their paintings.

As with the art shops and art galleries, so with the better theaters; one can choose to see excellent films of fantastic beauty. When we took our own children to see the finest and most inspiring films, it was surprising how we all came away exhilarated.

All of this entails a certain element of self-discipline. For those willing to take the time and thought to acquire wholesome viewing habits the whole of life can become brighter. And in the brightness the burdens of stress and strain are ever so much easier to bear.

12

The Magic of Music

There is in the Old Testament a strangely fascinating account about King Saul. He was the most handsome and outstanding man of his nation and was chosen to be its first king. For a while his reign prospered. With time, however, he became haughty, proud, and unwilling to obey God's commands.

Trouble and calamities began to come upon him. The worst of these were terrible moods of deep, dark depression. Nothing, it seemed, could possibly provide any sort of release until it was found that soft music could mend his troubled mind.

A decree was made to find the most skilled harp player in all the land and bring him to the palace. Eventually a young shepherd named David was chosen for his special musical talents. He came to the king's court to play. Then every time King Saul was troubled and downcast, David would play upon his harp and the dreadful depression would pass.

This true and touching story points up the magic there is in music, to relieve tension and heal the troubled mind.

The difficulty is that there is music and music. Like the old saying, "What is one man's meat is the other man's poison." Music that may mean a very great deal to one individual may produce nothing but revulsion in another. Symphonies and high-quality classical music may transport one person into raptures while the next-door neighbor is left absolutely unmoved. This difference can even exist in the same home between mother and father or parents and children.

So, what on the surface may seem a very simple subject to consider in taming tension suddenly shows itself to be quite complex. Only recently have truly advanced studies been made in the realm of sound and its impact on personality. Sophisticated research in the USSR has proven that with music it is possible to manipulate people like putty. Human personality can be built up, destroyed, distorted, or maddened by exposure to certain sounds, rhythms, and beats.

Though I am by no means an avowed pessimist, one aspect of the future which holds real foreboding for me is the possible manipulation of the masses by music. By the carefully calculated use of mass media combining certain types of apparently attractive programs with music of a certain caliber, it would be fairly easy to take captive entire communities. Human beings are perhaps more susceptible to the inducements of music than those of any other medium of communication. Nothing will so quickly produce certain positive responses in the human mind and emotions as music.

Music goes directly to the emotions and plays upon them with tremendous effect. Most of the time the listener may not even be aware that his or her emotions are even involved. Of course, if the music is of a soft and pleasing character, the listener may sense a mild feeling of contentment stealing over them. Or if it is martial music there may be a stirring of excitement within and the inclination to start marching. If the music carries a pronounced rhythm of lighthearted gaiety every person in the room may instinctively start to tap his toes on the floor or find his body swaying ever so slightly in time to the tune.

All of this demonstrates the direct effect of music upon us.

By exactly the same measure it can generate all sorts of destructive and damaging emotions. Again and again I have seen Africans worked up to fantastic frenzies by the persistent pounding of drums. The same sort of tensions are apparent in teen-age crowds carried away by various types of so-called "hip" music. In fact it has been said that an audience of ordinarily well-mannered young people can be utterly perverted in a matter of an hour of exposure to provocative music. Some authorities assert that all the restraints and conditioning of childhood can be canceled out by the malicious use of "mad" music in a matter of a few months.

If this is true of music as such, it is not hard to understand why some homes, instead of being happy havens of harmony, are instead fighting cockpits of terrible tension. Home after home becomes fragmented where the atmosphere is electric with high tension, stress, and strain. Even for visitors, time spent in such homes would be filled with enormous pressures. There would be intense personality conflicts, total lack of self-control, churlishness, outright hostilities, and mean moods.

It is not surprising that in almost every instance where this sort of tense environment exists the occupants are being assailed by a bedlam of wild music blaring from a record player, radio, or TV set. Even dogs or cats cannot cope with the cacophony and will slink away out the door for relief.

I clearly recall visiting in one home where our host had built his own hi-fi set. Whether or not he was hard of hearing I could not be sure. But the level at which he played the music day and night very nearly undid both my wife and me. At one point he asked us to sit in the center of the living-room sofa. Then he turned the set up to full volume and asked us if we could detect both the floor and walls vibrating. Both of us were so engrossed trying to keep our sanity we could scarcely do anything more.

One thing I do know: it was a distinct and positive relief to drive out of their yard and into the quiet countryside after a wearisome weekend of music.

The noise level at which much modern music is played is

part of the problem with people. The younger generation love their music loud. So, surprisingly, do more men than women. Therefore it follows that if either the father or children in a home control the volume of music it may well be very hard on the mother. I am convinced that one of the reasons why so many modern mothers are the harassed, crabby creatures they are is the mad music that beats upon their emotions from morning to night. The pity of it is that they become so used to it that even when they are alone they often forget to turn it down or, better still, turn it off.

Up to this point the entire question of music has been limited to the artificial sounds produced by human beings from various types of instruments and electronic gadgetry. But it must be realized that music in general also embraces all the natural sounds of the natural world. For instance, it takes in the singing of a meadowlark just as much as the rendition of a fine opera. It embraces the sighing of wind in the trees as much as the singing of a church choir. It includes the laughter of youngsters at play as much as a boy whistling his carefree tunes. It takes in the rumble of traffic and the roar of jets just as surely as the crash of breakers on the beach.

All of this is the music of the world around us. People will protest that this is not true. You may insist that I have widened the realm of music too far. But the simple fact is that music is sound and sound is music. What one loves another may hate.

There are men to whom the sweetest sound in all the world is a smooth-running internal combustion engine. Yet this is the same invention that now comes in for so much abuse because it pollutes the environment with both fumes and noise.

Louis Armstrong, the great black jazz player, was idolized around the world for the brassy blues he blew on his trumpet. But at the same time there are those who could not take ten minutes of his trumpeting.

Some people are lulled to sleep gently by the pounding rhythm of waves upon a beach. But others are driven to distraction by the eternal thump and thud of water crashing against land. More of those nights by the beach and they feel they will go berserk.

Consequently we are driven to the conclusion that music, or sound, if you will, is a most complicated subject. And since we live in a world where music, sound, noise, and commotion of all kinds assail us from all sides with increasing intensity, they produce their own pressures and tensions. The manner in which we react and respond to them determines the degree to which they either damage or refresh us.

It takes a certain amount of common sense combined with some serious thought to decide what we find helpful and what we find harmful. This chapter is, more than anything else, intended to stimulate some serious thought on the subject. It must be said in all seriousness as a solemn and sober warning that on the whole we are living in an increasingly noisy world. Noise pollution will no doubt be the last area of our environmental concern to be tackled seriously. Nonetheless it is now well substantiated that the average human being, even though conditioned to continuous noise, can still break down completely under its unrelenting assault. Some individuals can endure higher levels and greater intensity of sound than others. But ultimately the stresses and tensions experienced can produce deep-seated emotional and mental problems.

Ultimately what one has to do is to sit down quietly and discover exactly what it is one can tolerate happily. Each person has to decide what kind of sounds, what sort of music, soothes and relaxes him. He has to be earnest and sincere in his search to find what sort of noise actually does disturb him deeply and how to avoid it. Again this requires some thought and self-discipline, but the results may well be dramatic.

One winter my family and I were obliged to live in a very cramped suite. There were three other similar suites in the same building which had been so designed that the noise from the furnace room carried to every room. The disturbance of the heating unit going off and on was such that it played on people's nerves, made sleep difficult, and created very real tension among the tenants.

It became very clear that if we wished to enjoy a tranquil home environment we would have to find living accommodation elsewhere. Fortunately in the spring we found a larger house that was quiet and virtually noise-free. The entire change in the whole family was a revelation to me of just how much tension undue sound is able to generate.

But turning now to music in its more generally accepted form, there are certain basic suggestions which can be made that can prove helpful in most homes. The ideas I am sharing are not those of a dull old man with very specialized tastes in music. For in fact I love many kinds of music including the great classics, ballet, ensemble, string quartets, country music, folksongs, martial tunes, cowboy ballads, beautiful waltzes, and a great segment of sacred music.

What is more, I took both piano and violin lessons for years and play these instruments reasonably well. So again, I say that the remarks which follow are not just theoretical ideas about a subject which is foreign to me. Music has been a tremendous influence in my life. It has played a most important part in shaping my whole outlook.

It is extremely helpful just to know that music can and does tame tension. Instead of turning to drugs or tranquilizers one can turn to songs and melodies, which do greater good. Again and again during my lonely years when I had no home of my own and lived in a foreign land, I would take out my violin and play it to ease the heartache and inner pain. An hour of music making would set my heart to singing again. As the tunes and melodies tumbled from my memory and went singing out through the strings, my mind was set free from fret, and I found I could laugh once more and face my forbidding world.

The same is true of singing, humming, or whistling. It has been well said, "You can't sing and worry at the same time!" Try it, and see what happens. We don't have to be famous tenors or outstanding sopranos to sing. But let us sing, both collectively and alone. Sometimes when my wife and I are driving long distances we will sing duets. It is such a joy, this sharing—it banishes weariness and adds zest and gaiety to living.

One of the happy habits my wife has is to sing while she is

busy about her housework. There is something utterly sublime about a home made warm by the cheerful songs of a
contented woman. No matter how tough the outside world
may seem, when one enters a home bright with singing half
the world's stress and strain evaporate like mist under the
impulse of sun. There is absolute magic in such music, and it
is a shame so very few know this serene and simple secret.

Even such a simple habit as humming or whistling can turn
a doleful day into one filled with new hope and good cheer.
Just the mental concentration required to recall a melody or
remember a long-forgotten tune can take our thoughts off
our troubles and transfer them to more noble themes.

If one feels that singing or whistling is not for him and
learning a conventional instrument is much too difficult, try
playing a mouth organ. In our travels both my wife and I
carry mouth organs which are easily packed yet can provide
hours of happy songs. They are ideal around a campfire, on a
picnic, or at any informal occasion where bulkier instruments
are a bother.

One of the great gifts of modern technology to the twentieth century is the whole field of musical reproductions. Be it
long-play records, stereo, or tape recordings, the possibilities
have become so enormous and the cost is so low that almost
anyone can afford to have some of the world's finest music at
his finger tips.

Music made by others is never quite as beneficial as that
which originates within ourselves. Even the most homespun
song or roughest tune that tumbles out of a soul does some
deep good far beyond merely listening to another's work.
Still this is not to depreciate the work and artistic talent of
professional performers. Such music can play an important
role in our lives. It can give us enormous pleasure and also
serve to ease the tensions of life.

It is wise to cultivate a wide range of interests in music. Not
only does this add depth to our delight in music but gives us
bridges to common ground with other listeners. Nor should
we be afraid to expose ourselves to high-class music which
otherwise we might shun. There is a gradual unfolding of our-

selves as we do this. We find new insights that were not possible before, and we are lifted out of the old ruts and routines of listening.

Listening to different types of music need not be a dull or demanding routine. It can really be a very great adventure. I remember how for a long time I tended to shrink back from and almost abhor the ponderous work of Handel's *Messiah*. No one had ever taken the time to really explain it or its message to me. One day, while I was very ill in bed, a young Japanese neighbor, who was a great music enthusiast, came over with an armful of his favorite records. Among them was one in which the world-famous contralto Kathleen Ferrier sang some excerpts from the *Messiah*.

"You will really love this one," my neighbor commented. "She sings so clearly you get every word." And I did. In fact the message came through so beautifully that it completely broke down my resistance to the *Messiah*.

Eventually I purchased a complete album of the *Messiah* with a folio giving the full text of its songs. Gradually I gained full insight into the marvel and majesty of this inspired work, so much so that it was played over and over, not just at Christmas, but all year round. Perhaps no other single work so inspires me now as does this. At times when I am downcast or despondent over life's sufferings, the melodies and message of this music, showing how Christ Himself also felt such grief and sorrow, have lifted me in a way that no other human agency could possibly have done.

Over and beyond all of this there is absolutely no doubt whatever that music can set the mood in a home. It is perfectly valid to assert that in those homes where good music is played regularly, there is an atmosphere of repose and tranquility which can transcend the turmoil of life. The ability of music to tame our tensions and quiet our emotional upheavals is beyond my capacity to express with mere pen and paper.

When our children retired in the evening we made it almost a habitual practice to play fine recordings of Beethoven, Brahms, Mozart, and Haydn. In course of time they would even ask for soft music of this sort to be played as they drifted off into dreamland. It was more than a soporific exercise. It was the preparation of mind and heart for sweet slumber. Subconsciously there filtered into their makeups a deep and abiding appreciation for fine music.

It is, of course, well known that music can be a most pleasant adjunct to meals. Any dinner eaten within the atmosphere of soothing melodies is both more pleasant and better digested. The music tends to quiet anxieties and allay arguments or other provocative conversations that could mar the meal.

In contradistinction, if we insist on filling our homes with "mad" music, if we turn up the volume until our heads throb, if we play discordant melodies with their provocative beat, if we listen to lewd songs and suggestive ballads based on either perverted sex or outright sadism, we are bound to generate some terrible tensions. We need not be surprised if our surroundings become electric and charged with chaos, stress, and outright hostilities.

The choice is ours what we will have. It demands a certain degree of intellectual fortitude to swim against the modern flood of pollution that is filling airwaves and music shops. But there are faint glimmers of hope that even the "hip" generation is reacting against the muck and mud which some have attempted to pass off as real music.

Finally there is the whole realm of natural, lovely music outside the confines of our own four walls. Not too many people are attuned to its sounds. But for those with ears to hear and the inclination to pause awhile, there is played upon this planet harmonies as old as eternity itself.

There are the rhythm of waves on sand and rock, the rustle of grass and leaves beneath the wind, the strains of birdsong flung freely into the sky, the babble of streams and brooks and rivers, the lowing of cattle and the bleating of sheep. These and a score of other sounds comprise the symphony of the countryside. They are there to ease the mind, quiet the soul, and thus rejuvenate anyone who takes the time and trouble to listen to their music.

Seek them if you seek serenity.

13

Developing
Wholesome Attitudes

Our minds can be absolute monsters. Our inner thoughts can be terrible tyrants. Our whole outlook on life and others can be colored by the attitudes we hold and the habits of thinking which we tend to cultivate.

It is rather frightening to find that many of us have never been encouraged, much less instructed, in the art of acquiring wholesome attitudes. We stumble and blunder through life, trampling on other people's toes and hurting their feelings with scarcely a thought as to the consequences. The result is that often we find ourselves a bit forsaken. We tend to think we are being ostracized. There creeps into our consciousness the idea that the world is against us and life is very tough.

All too often this is the tragic truth. We sow hate and we reap hate. We plant prejudice and we harvest prejudice. We give ill will and we get ill will. We pass out judgment and we get back judgment. We cultivate criticism and censure and wonder why others tear us to pieces. We specialize in self-interest and then moan because no one cares about what happens to us. We heap abuse on others and then rebel when the heat is turned on us. We ignore others and their interests and then complain if no one seems to show interest in us.

The outcome of such habits is to find ourselves living lonely, fearful, tense lives. We are afraid of people and we go through the years haunted by what might boomerang against us.

Not all of us have been endowed with the same sort of personalities. There are those fortunate individuals who from birth seem to have a happy knack of getting on well with others. They are blessed with pleasing, magnetic personalities which make them popular and sought after.

At the same time there are men and women who, through no fault of their own, have very difficult dispositions. Perhaps through heredity or adverse environmental influences in their formative years they are mean, malicious, or even belligerent.

There are also all sorts of people with innumerable fears, peculiar phobias, unusual aversions, and deep-rooted hostilities which complicate their lives. Because no one may ever have explained to them some of the very simple secrets for getting along with others, they go through life under tremendous handicaps. What might otherwise be pleasant experiences turn out instead to be unhappy interludes charged with cruel, crushing misunderstandings.

This book is not meant to be a profound treatise on psychology or psychiatry. No attempt is made to diagnose or determine why people do the devilish things they do. Suffice it to say that this is simply so. What matters at this point is to present a few simple, positive steps which can be taken to improve our outlook and help us get along with others in an amicable manner.

Much of the tension and a great part of the worry in our lives revolve around friction with other human beings. Once we learn a few secrets to reducing this "rub," we will be amazed how it is quite possible to live a fairly serene life even with difficult people around us.

Perhaps the most important initial step is to recognize, and fully grasp, three cardinal concepts about human behavior. The first is that it is well-nigh impossible for me to change another person's personality. I may see (or think I see) all sorts of faults and flaws in his makeup which I feel need correction. But really, when all is said and done, there is virtually nothing I can do to alter them. The impact of my own character and conduct may have a great influence on others for good or evil. But basically I cannot change them to suit my fancy. God can and He does, by His Spirit, correct the faults in others, if we pray earnestly for them. Still the fact stands that I cannot change another to fit my particular likes or dislikes.

So then, if I am to get along with others I must accept them as they are. It is ever so simple to write this on paper. It is even easier to read it from the page. But it is perhaps the hardest thing to do in actual practice. This is the second, absolutely essential step to success with people. We simply must take them as they are. We must accept them completely with their weaknesses as well as their strengths. We must recognize that like ourselves they have lights and shadows to their characters and so we should expect no more from them than from ourselves. The moment we do this without any desire or intent of trying to change them, the tension between us disappears.

Suddenly it seems both they and I can drop our guards. We can be open, free, and honest in each other's presence. We can simply relax and enjoy our contact with each other.

The third concept is almost as important as the first two. Namely, I must acknowledge that even I am not perfect. Strange how many of us feel we are faultless! But the human being who is brave enough to take a hard, honest look at his own character without prejudice is well on the way to success in human relations. He will immediately see and admit that he has faults, weaknesses, and peculiarities which are hard on other people.

Once a person admits his faults, the next amazing discovery is that he can *do* something about them. While it is hopeless to try to change others, it is perfectly possible to alter ourselves. It is within our own power to shape and mold our own inner attitudes of mind if we are determined to do it.

There are some who will insist that this is not so. They contend it is like trying to lift yourself by your own bootstraps. I heartily disagree. This is the argument of the lazy individual who is content to drift through life without direction or self-discipline.

Were it otherwise, I would not have written this chapter. I do not indulge in double talk. And when I say that it is perfectly possible for people to develop wholesome attitudes in life, I mean just that. The trouble is that precious few feel their present attitudes are wrong. Or if they recognize that their attitudes are wrong they do not know *how* to alter them. They feel they are the helpless victims of heredity, environment, or circumstances. They think they are bound to go on through life with the same sort of behavior that necessarily produces tension, friction, and ill will with others.

This simply is not so. If they want to change, they can. That in itself is half the secret!

Now that this has been settled, where does one start? We start with the only place we can—ourselves. And what do we do with ourselves? Forget *self* for a spell. Not easy to do! After all, from earliest childhood "I" has been the very center of my world, the very center about which all of life revolved. My consuming interest, concern, passion, and preoccupation has been *me*.

Is it any wonder others get fed up with *me*—especially if that is really all I ever think about, talk about, or consider?

Let's set out deliberately to forget *me* at least for a part of each day. Let's try to put ourselves into somebody else's shoes for a spell. Let's try to see life through his eyes. Let's live in his little world for a while. If we do we will suddenly be surprised to see the good in his character. For the first time we may begin to really appreciate the sterling qualities that enable him to cope with his harsh circumstances in a way which we now realize we could never do. We realize that this other person has inner resources which we knew nothing about, and we will begin to appreciate what before we were inclined to criticize.

This ability to put ourselves in another's place is one of the great secrets to serene human relations. I have noticed all through life that the person who most quickly wins my confidence, trust, and friendship is the one who can best identify with me. The moment he shows enough interest to enter intimately into my situation, to walk in my sandals, to sit in my seat, to hoe my row in life—he has won my heart.

Doing this deliberately and thoughtfully automatically eases the strain and tames our tensions over other people's actions and activities. It clears up otherwise difficult misunderstandings. By putting myself in their place I can often see clearly exactly why they behave the way they do and say the things they do. I no longer sit on the sidelines, so to speak, passing judgment on the way they play the game of life. Now I am actually down on the same ground with them and I can grasp better why they do what they do.

Make no mistake—it is much easier to be a critical spectator in the arena of life than an active participant in other people's problems. This active entry into and personal identification with another's problems is a demanding art and it takes time to learn to play our part well. But when we do we will have found the way into a hundred hearts.

Another tremendously important point is a secret I did not discover until I was nearly fifty years of age. It is this. Many of us do not really understand ourselves. We do not understand why we think as we do, why we react as we do, why we say what we do, why we behave as we do.

We human beings are enormously complex. Our minds and personalities and characters are shaped and influenced both by heredity and all the influences of a lifetime. Ten thousand different impacts have been made upon us, shaping our lives. Some of these have been so subtle, so obscure, we did not even realize they were at work on us. But there they were, and we are the net product of myriad forces. If our actions and attitudes are an enigma to ourselves, then it can be understood why at times we baffle others.

It is this reason which in part led our Lord on Calvary to cry out from the depths of His heart, "Father, forgive them, for they know not what they do!" It was in part Christ's amazing insight into human behavior that enabled Him to make this plea for their forgiveness. The other part, of course, was His knowledge of the magnanimous character of God, His knowledge that out of God's love, compassion, and mercy for these men, forgiveness would be granted.

The point I am making here is that once we are big enough to realize that many men and women really do not know why they do what they do, our attitude toward them will alter. We move at once from a position of censure, criticism, and judgment to one of pardon, compassion, and concern.

The thrilling thing about this secret is that it sets both others and ourselves free in a new dimension of human relations. No longer do they try to justify their conduct nor offer all sorts of excuses to cover up their actions; instead they simply relax. For our part the hostility and antagonism which we would ordinarily entertain against them is dissipated by a deeper understanding that is the essence of compassion. Now instead of hating or despising them we sense a feeling of empathy and concern. This produces an immediate response of appreciation from them and the tension between us is gone.

Put in another way, they feel forgiven, they feel understood. And the wondrous thing about forgiveness and acceptance is that they always bring healing and soothing. They tame tension between two people as nothing else can ever do.

This acceptance of other people as they are has a remarkable liberating influence on ourselves. It sets us free from inner inhibitions, fears, and anxiety. We discover that it is possible to face life with good cheer, goodwill, and an open, generous attitude. We do not dread the stranger or shrink from strange situations. We sense a new attitude of wholesomeness towards the whole wide world.

This becomes particularly pronounced in the area of making friends and meeting new people. So many of us are afraid that we will be snubbed if we speak to strangers. We live within our own tiny shell, half hoping someone might be bold enough to break through it and embrace us with good-will; but we are afraid to do the same for someone else. If we remind ourselves that at one time our dearest and closest friends now were formerly strangers, we quickly see that it is merely fear of the unknown that holds us back. And if in the past we found that strangers can become friends, why not again and again?

The only single credential any man or woman needs to make friends is sincerity. It takes a very tough, self-important person not to respond to someone who shows a sincere interest in him and what he is doing. The great secret to gaining another's goodwill is to be sincere in our interest in that person.

The moment the stranger senses that he can please us by telling us a little about himself or his work or home or family, a bridge has been built between two people. For instinctively all of us want to give another person pleasure.

Giving another person the opportunity to provide pleasure is the greatest gift one can bestow upon another. This seems a complicated idea at first. It is one of those rather elusive principles which is even difficult to put down on paper. It is so obscure that some people live most of their lives without ever discovering it. They have missed half the secret to living!

This whole approach is so important I wish to develop it a bit further, because it is one of the truly sublime secrets to taming tension between ourselves and others.

Let me put it this way. Some of our "giving" in life is quite selfish and self-centered. If we are totally honest we will admit that much of the giving we bestow on others is simply in order to get back a certain amount of approval and appreciation from them. To be quite blunt, we give in order to get. Of course it is absurd to say this is always so; the world is much blessed with big-hearted people who give solely out of generous impulses.

But over and beyond this there is an even more magnanimous attitude by which we deliberately provide others with the pleasure of giving pleasure. This is why, for instance, we find very often that if we are in dire need of help, and pocket our pride and ask for help, we are overwhelmed by how readily even a stranger will respond. It gives him enormous satisfaction to be able to assist. He is given a great deal of joy by being in a position to help. This idea of "feeling wanted," of "feeling useful," of "being able to give pleasure to another," will win the hardest heart.

When I was a very young man I learned this lesson in dealing with a most difficult neighbor. I had been warned, when I moved into the district, that he was an eccentric recluse who tried to keep the whole world at arm's length. He was not interested in strangers and during all the years he lived in the district never made a fast friend. Being his closest neighbor, I soon realized I could not live at a distance even if he wanted to do so.

One day some of his cattle crawled through the fence into my fields. When I took them back to his yard, I noticed an amazing array of tools, machines, and other equipment around his shed. At once I knew that engines were his first love and no doubt he was an excellent mechanic. I passed a few casual comments about this and then left. The dour owner scarcely spoke.

It was some time later that my tractor broke down. I decided then and there was the time to break the ice between my neighbor and me. Putting my personal pride aside, I walked over to his little farm and found him up in a cherry tree, picking fruit. "Norm," I began, "I'm in deep trouble—my tractor has quit and nothing I can do will make it start!" He seemed to ignore me and went on picking cherries. "I believe you must really understand engines inside out. Do you think you could get my tractor started for me?"

Almost before I realized what had happened, he slipped down out of the tree, went over to his garage, and came back with a box of tools. "Sounds like ignition trouble to me," he mumbled. "Let's go see."

Together we worked on the tractor until nearly midnight. When it finally fired up and began to run smoothly, his stern face was wreathed in smiles. He would not take a cent for his trouble. But I had won a firm friend for life. That was over twenty-five years ago, and we still enjoy each other's visits and correspondence. Norm turned out to be the truest neighbor I ever had. Again and again he came to my rescue, and each time he did, it seemed to weld our friendship deeper. He was being given the opportunity he needed in his austere life to help someone else, to provide another with pleasure. And it made him my friend.

Most of us in our relationships with others are too proud, too self-important, too independent. We proceed on the basis that we don't want to bother others, when actually they ache and hunger down inside for a chance to do something for someone. So if we want to spread a bit of sunshine and endear ourselves to people, perhaps the greatest secret is for us to just let ourselves go, pocket our pride, forget ourselves, and become available to others.

Again and again I have noticed that the secret to the success of some people is their total lack of pretense and front. They are willing to drop in on someone and thus give him the pleasure of providing them with a meal or a clean bed and bath.

One of my best-loved friends has the happy knack of doing this. He suddenly shows up at the door. There is no fuss, no formality, no prior or worried preparation. He simply shares what we have, and it is such a pleasure to do this for him. This is his happy secret to having a whole host of friends all over the country. His coming creates only pleasure and not anxiety.

Another simple secret which is very ancient but often forgotten is treating others as we wish to be treated. If we expect others to be prompt, then we should be prompt; if we wish them to be courteous, then we should be courteous; if we feel they should be generous, then we should be generous. It is fairly true to say that in life we generally get back what we give. And the way in which we treat others will be somewhat reflected in the way they treat us.

If we are tense, nervous, suspicious, and on edge with others, we often find the same sort of response from them. If we spread an attitude of ease and gaiety and good cheer, it is more than likely to produce a corresponding reaction in others. Naturally I have lived too long to say that this will always work, but it certainly does not hurt to try. When we do our part, we have at least peace of mind in the matter, and that is a great gift to possess.

Then lastly there is the simple, old art of giving happiness to others. One of the great writers of the last century once made the comment that "it is a solemn thing to realize that we hold another's happiness in our hands." What have I done this day? What have I said this day? What have I written? Where have I gone? What have my attitudes been in these past twenty-four hours to add to the sum total of happiness for others?

If I truly care about the world's becoming a more wonderful place in which to live, if I am earnest in my desire to add to the contentment of society, if I am keen to make others happy, if I am aiming to tame tension, I shall live to help someone today.

14

Social Behavior

Before we leave our study of the mental and emotional pressures which assail us, it might be useful to examine some of the reasons for our social behavior. Very often if we understand why humans behave as they do, we are better able to accept their actions and attitudes. Not only does this relieve our own tensions and hostilities, but also those of others around us.

It has been stated several times already that we all tend to fear the unknown. Whenever we are confronted by unusual behavior or unfamiliar attitudes, we are inclined to put up our guard and tense ourselves for any eventuality. This defensive reaction on our part can and generally does generate a similar response from the stranger. Immediately, then, we are all under stress—that is to say, social stress.

It is not generally known that in any given group of animals—be they birds, cattle, sheep, or human beings—there is what is known as the "pecking order" or "horning order" or "butting order" or "social standing." This arrangement of individuals within the group from top to bottom in a definite sequence of priority is a most powerful social impulse. It operates continuously. It really is part of the old jungle order, the law of survival of the fittest. By sheer strength of purpose and self-assertion each member of the group finds the level within the context of its surroundings where it can best survive. The most aggressive members are at the top, the least so at the bottom.

This order, unfortunately, is never static. As the strengths and weaknesses of the various members fluctuate, so does their standing, for there is continual competition to be "top dog," so to speak. Beyond this there are always bound to be some individuals dropping out and new ones entering. This adds to the continuous rivalry, for each newcomer endeavors at once to establish some sort of advantageous position in the pile.

If one studies this subject in a pen full of chickens or a herd of cattle or flock of sheep, it is almost a painful process to watch, the more so if our sympathies lie with the weaker ones who are continuously bunted, horned, or pecked into submission.

In human behavior the same rivalries, tensions, stress, and anxiety are at work. They are, however, less clearly comprehended, simply because of our cunning ability to cover up our attitudes and actions. We are conditioned from childhood to be reasonably polite and courteous even in conflict with others. Added to this is the false front so many wear to mask their true motives.

Because of this, human social behavior becomes exceedingly complex. People feel and know they are under tremendous tension; they sense the stresses and strains of their social lives; they are aware of the anxieties and worry of trying to get ahead. But in spite of all this they really don't understand why, much less how to meet the menace.

In the struggle for social acceptance and success, a great many good people go to the wall. The effort and energy expended to "keep up with the Joneses" exhaust them with unutterable weariness and endless worry.

So it must be asked, is there any way to cope with conflicts? Is there any sane, simple, sensible manner in which these tensions can be tamed?

Yes, there is, but it requires a certain degree of mental fortitude to do it.

For one thing the formula is not too palatable for most of us. It goes against the grain and rubs us the wrong way. It can best be summed up in one word which we don't hear much about anymore—"humility."

The proud person, the self-important individual, is bound to resent this. In fact most of us are so stubborn on the point we prefer to live with our pride and pay the penalty of terrible tension. Rather than be humble we will hold on to our haughty self-esteem and endure endless stress and strain because of it.

Somehow we simply cannot believe or accept the idea that it is the place of least prominence that offers the greatest peace. Always we have imagined that serenity was to be found only at the summit. And to attain the pinnacle of power, prestige, and position, we will literally drive ourselves and others to desperation.

I would like to give a very personal, painful, but pointed illustration of precisely what I mean. It may help to set someone else's thoughts on a more rewarding and easier way of living.

As a young man I was an exceedingly ardent automobile driver. I prided myself on my ability to drive hard, fast, and relentlessly on any sort of road. Over the course of several years I established time records for traveling long distances under the most hazardous driving conditions. With the passing of time I became increasingly arrogant and aggressive on the highways. I could not rest a moment if I saw a car ahead of me. I simply had to pass it, I had to show my imagined superiority, I had to prove I was "top dog" on the road.

The result was that I lived under terrible tension. Any time I drove I was under excessive stress. Because my job as a crop inspector all over the country involved driving about a thousand miles a week, I literally lived under endless strain.

About this time I married. Immediately my lovely young

bride sensed the strain under which I drove. Again and again she begged me to let up. But my pride and prowess would not relent. I had a reputation as a formidable driver, and I would not give it up. Instead I tried even harder to maintain and surpass my records. The result was that both my wife and I were brought under increasing strain. Driving was not a delight; it was more like a very bad dream in which all that mattered was getting from A to B in the shortest time, no matter how dangerously. All I saw along the way was the winding pavement and the shining center line that held me mesmerized mile after mile.

Now the reader will say, "What a stupid fellow!" or think even more strongly, "Why didn't he have the sense to smarten up?"

Looking back now I fully agree that my conduct and actions and attitude on the highway were utter folly and madness. I was a victim of the "pecking order," and it took a terrible accident to wake me up.

One day, I was driving very hard and very fast, a short way behind another relentless driver. He suddenly swung out to pass the car in front of him and had a head-on collision with an oncoming vehicle. It happened before my eyes and I was the first one on the scene to lend assistance. It was my unpleasant and grisly task to try to lift one of the drivers out of his blood-spattered vehicle that looked like the interior of an abattoir. As gently as I could I laid him on the grass by the road, then raced to a nearby farm house to call an ambulance.

As I stooped over the dying driver there flashed into my awareness, for the first time, the realization that this might well have been me. Again and again in my stubborn pride I had endangered my own life and that of others by driving so very aggressively. It was a most humbling moment. In it I learned a lesson that has lasted all my life.

Since that day I have driven gently, contentedly, and sensibly. I have let all who wanted to pass me do so.

The amazing and wonderful thing is that suddenly driving became a tremendous delight. First of all the tension was gone and the stress on myself and my passengers was completely replaced with contentment. Secondly I began to really see the countryside, the city sights, and the other fascinating aspects of the world through which I traveled. In a new and wondrous way my driving brought a whole new dimension of beauty into life.

It has been well said that "the man already on the ground can fall no further." Learning to be bottom man on the totem pole always brings rich compensations with it. It is the person who puts himself up on a pedestal who is riding for a fall. The one willing to take a lower seat has learned to tame tension in any social setting.

This applies to all the multitude of rivalries, jealousies, and friction that develop in every human community. It is just as true in the office, industry, a social club, or a church group as it is in a home and family.

It is not natural or easy to humble ourselves. It is very much against our ego. Few of us seem able to learn this lesson from others. Sometimes it takes a tough, hard lesson to teach us this truth. It is necessary for people who really want to tame tension in their lives to take a long hard look at this subject. If they are intelligent they will weigh the advantages and disadvantages of aggressiveness and decide against it.

Another thought which can help us here is to realize that the majority of human beings are so selfish and so self-centered that they really don't care very much whether *you* succeed or not. They aren't too impressed by your position, prestige, or power. They may be jealous and envious, in which case you immediately feel threatened. But the vast majority really couldn't care less.

So, again, one must ask, Whom are you trying to impress? So much of the show, front, and trappings that people display either in what they own or how they act is intended to overwhelm others. Most of it fails utterly to do this. So why bother? Why live under stress needlessly?

Another powerful force invariably at work in any given group of animals is the need for space, room, or territory. Studies of wild animal behavior under stress have led to the discovery of some remarkable parallels in human communities where people are crowded and exposed to extreme population pressures. Especially is this true of those cramped or confined by large cities. Many modern sociological problems are now attributed to the tension of trying to live in a so-called ant-heap environment.

The rather sad and certainly subtle aspect of this dilemma is that people may not even know that they are under tension from this cause. If they experience anxiety, nervousness, instability, or a sense of being cramped, they really cannot account for it. Some individuals are so susceptible to this type of stress that they nearly panic under the pressure. Their behavior patterns may be considered decidedly antisocial and yet there appears outwardly to be no visible reason for it.

The classic illustration of this phenomenon is the suicidal behavior of lemmings in the arctic. When their populations reach unendurable proportions a sort of mob hysteria overtakes them. They begin to rush off blindly, en masse, no doubt seeking escape and release from their constricting pressures. They often end up plunging into the sea, drowning in rivers, lakes, and streams, as they swarm over the area, crazed by the sheer population pressures built up within the species. Then, once these pressures have been released and the numbers greatly reduced, the remnant return to normal.

In the case of human beings we simply do not give sufficient thought to the entire concept of space for living. Within the constricting confines of our metropolitan areas in particular, there is a tendency always to cram as many people as possible into as small a space as possible. Partly, this is because of the price of property and cost of providing accommodation. In the long run, however, this may well prove to be a poor sort of economy. For what is saved in one direction may be more than offset by the cost of providing social services to people who break down under the stress of our urban "pressure cooker" environment.

One can detect this same trend even in such areas as our modes of transportation or our recreational facilities. We crowd as many passengers as possible onto a plane, bus, or train. Or we pack as many ticket holders as we can into a theater, stadium, or concert hall. Even our homes, apartments, and offices become highly restricted areas in which elbow room is well-nigh nonexistent. One can hardly stretch out full length without poking someone else in the ribs.

It is not surprising then that a certain sort of quiet yet frantic desperation seems to settle over so many people. In a sense they feel trapped. Their jobs, home, or family may make it imperative for them to live in the mad bustle of the urban environment, but all the time they yearn to be set free, to wander loose. Of course, the tragedy is that many do not realize their dilemma. They may place the blame for their tenseness, anxiety, and nervous behavior on a dozen other things. To the end of their days they may be bedeviled by crowding and not know it. It is for this reason that it is important in city planning to provide the public with open spaces, parks, recreational areas, and greenbelts.

But none of these amenities are of any advantage unless people avail themselves of them. If we are to tame some of the tensions arising from crowding, then we have to take ourselves firmly in hand and seek out some quiet, secluded spot where we can be alone for at least a few minutes during the day. This is a tremendous tonic to nerves and minds tense with stress and strain from being surrounded by too many people.

At one stage of my early career I was forced to work in a very cramped office in the heart of a very large and very dirty city. At first I was quite sure the place would drive me to desperation. Having been born and raised in the great expanses of Africa's open plains and hills, cities of any kind were a terror to me. I simply loathed their confinement, and this was one of the worst.

Fortunately in this case I discovered a small park not far from the office where a few sickly roses tried to survive amid the smog and smoke of the industrial area. A few trees, too, managed to stay half alive in their polluted environment. At best it was a pathetic place, but it did have space. So every noon hour I would go there to be alone, eat my sandwiches, and saunter up and down under the cloud-shrouded sun. This was all that kept me from breaking down under the bondage of the cramped and crowded quarters where I worked.

Happily, it was not long before my company moved me to a new place of responsibility on a large ranch out in the cattle country. I felt like a bird being set free from the restrictions of an iron cage.

It is not always easy or possible to find a park or piece of open ground where one can be alone. In this case it helps just to take a walk alone, even though others may be using the sidewalks. And failing that, at least go into a room where you can shut the door and be by yourself, away from the presence and impact of other people. This is especially beneficial for mothers who have their families around them continuously. Lack of privacy is one of the reasons some object strongly to open-plan homes. All of us instinctively and subconsciously for our own mental and emotional well-being demand some time and space where we can be free of human pressures upon us.

If there are no convenient opportunities to be alone outdoors, then a den or other secluded space should be supplied in the home. There must be a place one can go to be alone for a little while each day. We are each entitled to the benefit of being left by ourselves for a spell to think over our thoughts, relax from the relentless pressures upon us, and have a chance to breathe deeply of a few minutes' freedom from other human beings.

Strange to say, extensive research into human conduct among prison inmates has shown that all people have an invisible sort of "privacy perimeter" around them. It is larger in back of us than in front, simply because we are aware of people approaching from in front, whereas we cannot see what sneaks up behind. In animal behavior this is referred to as the "attack radius." The moment another approaches too close for our comfort we become tense and alert. This characteristic of human conduct also generates tension in a crowded situation. It explains why in many cases we will hear people cry out, "Don't touch me!" or "Can't you leave me alone?" or "What do you want again?" or "Must you always hang around me?"

All of these denote a deep inner detestation of being approached too closely or too often. The subconscious response is to keep at arm's length whoever is not very dear or well known to us. This also explains why the extended and open handshake between strangers is such a singularly significant gesture. I am reaching out beyond my normal privacy perimeter to make deliberate contact with another.

Understanding the fundamental forces at work here helps us to understand ourselves and why we often react as we do. Such understanding should assist us to take common-sense, intelligent steps to ease our tensions.

For example, another excellent idea is to slip away every other weekend to some favorite secluded spot where one can be alone. It is not wise to always take guests along, as many do. Nor is it wholesome to think one can have a good time only by mingling with a crowd, some of whom one may never have met before. Actually this often only sets up new tensions and can duplicate the complexities of the city which were left behind.

Of course, in all of this, there has to be maintained a sense of balance in human behavior. I am not advocating that we should become recluses. But for the man or woman who feels harassed and jaded by the relentless pressures of other people, some spells of utter privacy can be a precious tonic.

There is another aspect to human pressures which should be touched on before ending our thoughts about mental and emotional problems. It has to do with personality traits.

Some of us wonder why it is that we seem to "hit it off" with some folks, while others really rub us the wrong way from the moment we meet them. In the office, at work, in the home, in our clubs, at school, anywhere that human beings are brought together, this question of personality conflict arouses tremendous tensions.

Again it is very important for us to realize why such conflicts arise, what causes them, and probably most important, how to cope with their destructive forces that can generate so much stress and strain in any given situation.

Generally speaking, human personalities fall naturally into four rather distinct categories or classifications. The *choleric* person is inclined to be hot-headed, fiery-tempered, impulsive, quick-minded, alert, able to make decisions on the spot, active, and aggressive, with great ambitions and energy to achieve them. He or she is generally a leader or organizer.

The *phlegmatic* person is almost the opposite. A very quiet, unruffled sort of individual, easy-going, soft-spoken, with a tranquil disposition. If anything, he is inclined to be a bit indolent or lazy, willing to let others take the lead and make decisions. He is not easily aroused or excited, but generally very dependable.

The *melancholic* person is the introvert, the one who is inclined to take life seriously. Many great thinkers, scholars, and artists have this makeup. They are inclined to be moody, melancholy at times, and even morbid. Often they have brilliant minds, are highly gifted, and yet find difficulty in reaching out to others around them. Sometimes they are very solitary souls.

The *sanguine* person is the happy-go-lucky, lighthearted character who always sees the silver lining to every cloud. He is an inveterate optimist. His good nature spills over easily into other lives. He is often a popular person who loves people. Yet because of his very easygoing manner and "hail fellow well met" outlook he often lacks depth, sincerity, or purpose. He may be inclined to be long on promises but short on performance.

Naturally these are but thumbnail sketches of the four main personalities found in people. They do not constitute exhaustive definitions. But they are sufficient for the reader to identify with one of them more readily than the others. Few individuals fit precisely into any one of these categories. Most of us have predominantly one of these types of personality in combination with one or more of the others to a lesser degree. For example, it is quite common to find a truly choleric individual with some strong sanguine traits.

But the important thing is to see that we do have different personalities. And beyond this we should understand that very often two people of the same type tend to repel rather than attract each other. When we put two very melancholic people together, we can be quite sure they will soon be singing the blues; or if two choleric individuals are thrown side by side, we can expect fireworks and explosions.

Just grasping these basic behavior patterns can do wonders to reduce personality conflicts and ease the tensions among us. As we learn to study, watch, and analyze others as well as ourselves we will appreciate why we can make enduring friendships with some whereas others simply repel us. In this knowledge not only is there a certain sense of fun and adventure, but also a deep degree of sympathetic understanding for other people. Instead of criticizing, condemning, or denouncing their behavior we can appreciate in a mature manner why they behave as they do.

For the fact remains that half the secret to truly successful living is learning to get on with other people in an atmosphere of peace and goodwill. And once we understand personality problems we will be much less afraid of others. We can relax and let down our guard, thus easing the strains and tensions which otherwise attend personality conflicts.

If we add to all of this the simple but profound formula of actually searching out the good in our fellow human beings, most of our anxieties will disappear. This is stated in utter sincerity without any attempt to be the least bit sanctimonious.

Not only should we look for the good in others, but we should be courageous enough to compliment them on their good traits. We should not be afraid to give encouragement to our fellow travelers on the rocky road of life. One of the great secrets to serene living is to recall the good, noble, kind, and generous things others have done for us, then to turn around and thank them. It will rekindle their desire to do even better and bind them to us with increasing affection. It never fails.

PART THREE

Spiritual Life

15

Knowing God

There are men and women who may have succeeded well in every realm of living except their spirits. They may have attained wealth, power, prestige, and popularity, yet be poor in spirit. It is significant of the twentieth century that despite our increased affluence, greater leisure, and longer life with all of its technological advances, mankind is more restless and dissatisfied than ever before. Regardless of all that money, science, research, and sociological studies can do, the inner heart hungers for more than just materialistic answers to the questioning spirit.

This inner longing, this quest for purpose to living, is one of the greatest tensions of our times. Yet there is really nothing new about this inner restlessness of the human heart. From earliest times it has been with men.

Augustine, the ancient seer of North Africa, put it in a nutshell when he wrote: "Oh God, thou hast made us for thyself, and our hearts are restless, searching till they find their rest in thee."

That the search goes on cannot be denied. Everywhere

men seek solace for the tension within. They turn to every conceivable sort of teaching, philosophy, religion, or mysticism for meaning to living. Many, like derelict ships adrift, are swept hither and yon on the changing tides of thought and learning. There is no direction to their course. They sense this lack of direction and they fear the future.

So it is proper for us to ask the simple question, "Is it really possible to find inner peace and tranquility? Is there something or someone that can help us tame these inner tensions? Is there a rest to be found for our restless, questioning spirits?"

The answer is yes! As Augustine put it so precisely, "Our hearts are restless, searching till they find their rest in thee."

It is possible to find God. It is, moreover, possible to really know Him in a personal and intimate manner. By this I am not implying that one finds religion, or knows *about* God. What I am saying is much more direct than that. I am saying it is perfectly possible to enter into a personal, firsthand acquaintance with God. Then once we have met Him, it is possible to have this introduction grow into a very deep and enduring friendship. But beyond even this there is the sublime sense in which we come to feel a part of the family of God: He is in fact a Father to us and we are His contented children. And it is in this context that great serenity sweeps over our lives. We know where we belong at last. We have come home. The wandering is over. The search is ended. The soul is at rest.

The difficulty is that a lot of very sincere people do not believe this is possible. They claim it is self-delusion. Like Karl Marx they insist it is like an opiate with which one can be drugged. But the truth is just the opposite. To those who have found God and know Him, He is the most meaningful person in life. He alone brings order and purpose out of what otherwise would be chaos and confusion.

Whether we wish to admit it or not, we live amid a confusion of thought. This chaos creates enormous turmoil in our times and brings in its train a whole host of tensions and anxieties. Therefore it must follow that if we can find and come to know one who is able to give clear direction to us in our dilemma, the anxieties will evaporate. We will know where we are going and in that knowledge and assurance we shall find peace of heart and quietness of mind.

How then do we get to know God? How do we find Him? How can we make contact? Where do we go to get an introduction?

Strange to say, and this may startle many readers, He is and has been even more anxious to meet us. He has gone to great lengths to insure that we can get to know Him.

He has chosen to show Himself to us in four ways. We must recognize, of course, that God is no mere person. It is true He has personality, He has character, He is capable even of assuming our humanity, but He is not a mere human being. He is also infinite in all of His attributes. Because of this, though able to identify with us, He is far beyond us and therefore deserving of our deepest respect and devotion.

He has deigned to reveal Himself to us in rather simple yet effective ways. They are simple enough that an untutored savage or even a small child can understand. Yet they are effective enough to elicit a response from the most brilliant mind and highly developed intellect, provided that intellect is not blinded and bigoted by its own pride and self-importance.

Here are the four ways to knowing God.

First of all He has given to us a concept of His character in the natural and created universe which He brought into being. The beauty and brilliance of flowers, trees, birds, skies, clouds, grass, hills, mountains, streams, sun, moon, stars, and ten thousand other forms of animals, insects, plants, and fishes are utterly beyond the mind of man to explain. It is not enough to say they are the product of physical and biological forces working by blind impulse or mere whimsy. The order, unity, and obvious thoughtful design that run through every segment of the universe speak eloquently of a master mind and indulgent creator. There is nothing casual or random about it. It all functions with meticulous precision and meaningful progress. It all denotes careful planning with a specific purpose in mind.

All that is noble and fine in our own human cultures and society must make us pause and wonder about the natural world. Our own responses to the song of a bird, the graceful motion of a swan, the glory of a sunrise or sunset, are more profound than the mere interaction of chemicals or reaction of our bodies to physical stimuli.

Something within our own spirits answers to the divine spirit in quiet assurance that all of this beauty and design and order are a part of His character and mind. To repudiate them is to ignore God. To deliberately shut our souls to this self-disclosure by God is to refuse to accept His overtures to us.

Paul, the great thinker and mighty intellect of the early Christian era, put it this way in rather blunt but unmistakable language:

> Since the beginning of the world the invisible attributes of God, for example, his eternal power and divinity, have been plainly discernible through things which he has made and which are commonly seen and known, thus leaving these men without a rag of excuse. They knew all the time that there is a God, yet they refused to acknowledge him as such, or to thank him for what he is or does. Thus they became fatuous in their argumentations, and plunged their silly minds still further into the dark. [Romans 1:20-21 (J. B. Phillips)]

The very reason why many people today find it impossible to attain peace of heart is that they deliberately refuse to admit that God even exists. We must face the fact that it takes two people to have friendship. It takes two people to establish a Father-child relationship. And if one of the parties persists in deliberately denying that the other one exists, not even acknowledging that He is alive, how can one possibly hope for a meeting? How can there be any contact? How can any acquaintance even commence?

I am aware that, especially for the intellectually sophisticated person, it requires pocketing one's pride to look for God in the natural world. But He is there, waiting quietly and patiently to meet the open heart and open mind. And when He does, He always brings peace.

Secondly, we can know God through the lives and personalities of other people. Almost all of us at some time or another in life have encountered individuals who are entirely different from other people. There is a unique spirit of goodwill, wholesomeness, and warmhearted generosity about them. Very often we are surprised to discover that they have not always been like this, that at some point in their past there has been a direct encounter between them and God. He has entered into their lives in a most intimate manner. The result was a complete change of conduct and alteration of attitudes.

There is something intensely attractive about the spirit of these people. They are serene, tranquil, and joyous in a dimension that does us great good. It is a pleasure to be with them and sense the love and character of God in their lives.

I clearly recall the first stranger of this sort I ever met. I had been sent 250 miles away from home at the age of eight to attend a boarding school. Naturally I felt torn up about it. The big, rambling, barnlike building where we were housed and taught seemed a gloomy, dark, cold, forbidding place. Most of the staff struck me as being a stiff crowd of rather cruel characters. Certainly their conduct did little for a small lad, far from home and quite frightened by this grim and austere world.

Only the principal was a different sort of person. She was a tiny, misshapen, homely little lady who had never known good health. Her back was hunched, her arms and legs were scrawny, her face was plain, her straight hair was pulled back in a tight bun.

But we boys and girls scarcely saw these characteristics at all. Instead there radiated from within this little bundle of humanity so much love, so much warmth, so much downright goodness, so much sweet serenity and contentment that we were drawn towards her in a dramatic way. So much did we love this woman that we boys would actually fight each other just for the favor of carrying home her briefcase of books. Some of us have corresponded with her continuously for over forty years. Her life is still speaking for God.

Her secret was simple. She knew God. She loved Him. She

walked and talked with Him. She reflected His character to us children. And many of us came to know Him because we first saw what He was really like through her life.

The third way in which it is possible to know God is through His own self-revelation in writing. A great deal has been written down through the long history of mankind to help us know God. From earliest times those men and women who had intimate contacts with Him attempted to express their insights by both the spoken and written language of their race.

There has, of course, been a certain degree of controversy as to how much of what was written was inspired. Yet the fact remains that sufficient has been put into human language to help any truly seeking heart to find and know God.

The greatest single compilation of divine revelation is contained within the small library of sixty-six books, written by some forty different authors over a period of 1,500 years, commonly called *the Scriptures* or *the Bible.* No other single source of written material has enabled so many men and women to know God. It has been read by millions of people in hundreds of languages all over the earth.

In addition to this collection of writings, which we accept as being inspired by the Spirit of God because of their unity, authenticity, and ability to change human lives, there is a great mass of other helpful material. There are sacred hymns, songs, and psalms. There are great sermons. There are devotional meditations. There are spiritual discourses by devout and godly thinkers. There are tracts, pamphlets, and numerous other regular publications to help people to *know God.*

Of course, studying the Scriptures themselves is the surest way to knowing God. It entails time, meditation, thought, prayer, and an open spirit that is not prejudiced with personal pride. The number of people who have learned to love God and know Him well in this way runs into many, many millions. This is especially true today when new translations in modern idiom make reading of the Bible so much more relevant.

I am prepared to say that anyone disturbed in spirit can

find ease of heart and mind in this book. Only one condition is required. The reader must come in humility, prepared to make the moral commitments and decisions which a diligent study will demand. Begin with the Gospel of John. It could well be the key to unlocking a whole new world of quiet joy and serene contentment for your spirit.

Finally, the fourth way in which we can know God is through the life and person of Jesus Christ. Most of our information about His life is contained in the New Testament, though other books concerning His teachings abound.

If I may be pardoned for saying so, there are really three Jesus Christs. I put it this way to be as plain and helpful as I can. But before I explain, may I make it abundantly clear that this person was not just a man. He was in absolute fact God in human form. He was the "God-man"—Jesus—the Christ.

There is first the historical Jesus Christ. He is best known to most people as a Jewish teacher who lived roughly twenty centuries ago in Palestine. He was accused of blasphemy by the ecclesiastical hierarchy and finally committed to crucifixion by the ruling Romans. To know this much about Him is not to know Him or to know God.

Secondly, there is the theological Jesus Christ. He is perhaps more obscure than the historical Jesus. He is held tenuously in the thinking of many great scholars, teachers, and even laymen as the propounder of profound truth. It is perfectly possible to be steeped in all of His teachings, to be able to dissect and debate His discourses, yet not really know Him or God.

Thirdly, there is the actual, living, Lord Jesus Christ. Though He once lived among us as a man, He is in fact God. His teachings were divine. His death was His own deliberate redemptive act on our behalf and in our stead. His bodily resurrection was positive evidence of His power over both death and decay. It is He who shattered for all time the shackles of both sin and death that bind the human heart. By His living Spirit He comes even now to reside within our spirits if we invite Him. It is He who sets us free from our anxieties and tensions. To know this Christ is to know God.

16

Faith: What It Is
and How It Works

Up to this point in the book a very deliberate effort has been made to discuss the subjects under consideration in a logical manner. No effort has been spared to appeal to the reason of the reader so that he may understand what forces produce tension either in the body or mind and how to counteract those influences.

But when we moved into the less well known and less familiar area of the human spirit in the preceding chapter, no doubt certain difficulties began to arise for some. The reader may have begun to feel a bit lost.

This is easy to understand. Most of us from our childhood have been conditioned to think in terms of only visible or tangible things. These we generally refer to as being "real." Somehow most of us are very much more at ease discussing or dealing with such solid subjects as our homes, family, friends, money, food, or clothing. A few people are bold enough to try to talk about abstract things like hope, love, joy, and peace, if they are pushed into it. But as a rule the majority shy away from such subjects simply because it seems in no time they are a bit beyond their depth. Even though love, joy, faith, and sincerity may play important roles in their lives, they do not discuss them except on rare occasions and then only in confidence with a close friend.

When we move out beyond this realm to the region of our relationship to God, who is Spirit, we almost always find people are even more unsure of themselves. In a peculiar way they become almost paralyzed. It is as if spiritual matters are quite beyond them. They act as if this were an area of discussion entirely out of this world.

In a way this is exactly so. It is not that matters of the spirit are of no consequence in life. Quite the opposite—they are of paramount importance. Rather, the difficulty is in trying to use our logic and reason to grasp ideas which are essentially of the spirit and beyond the bounds of mere human intellect.

Paul, perhaps the greatest intellect of his time, explains this very clearly in his first letter to the young church at Corinth:

> God has, through the Spirit, let us share his Secret. For nothing is hidden from the Spirit, not even the deep wisdom of God. For who could really understand a man's inmost thoughts except the spirit of the man himself? How much less could anyone understand the thoughts of God except the very Spirit of God? And the marvelous thing is this, that we now receive not the spirit of the world but the Spirit of God himself, so that we can actually understand something of God's generosity towards us.
>
> It is these things that we talk about, not using the expressions of the human intellect but those which the Holy Spirit of God himself, so that we can actually understand something of God's generosity towards us.
>
> But the unspiritual man simply cannot accept the matters which the Spirit deals with—they just don't make sense to him, for, after all, you must be spiritual to see spiritual things. The spiritual man, on the other hand, has an insight into the meaning of everything, though his insight may baffle the man of the world. This is because the former is sharing in God's wisdom. . . . Incredible as it may sound, we who are spiritual have the very thoughts of Christ. [I Corinthians 2:10-16 (J. B. Phillips)]

In light of this I believe it is fair and appropriate to say that in order to grasp spiritual facts we must pass beyond the realm of logic and reason to that of faith. Of course at this point many very sincere people will insist that human intelligence is sufficient to untangle the tightest knots of life. They will declare vehemently that anything outside the frame of reference of human logic is pure wishful thinking. They will want to dismiss the entire spiritual realm with a casual shrug because it is not subject to the basic scientific approach of observable phenomena.

I admit quite freely and frankly that for such people there really is very little use in reading on any further in this book. If they are being absolutely sincere and utterly honest in their contentions that no spiritual realm exists, or that if it does, it is most definitely on the periphery of life and not at its center, then what follows simply will not make sense.

But if the reader, at any time, has experienced even the tiniest hint of an inner longing, a peculiar pull toward a higher power than himself or herself, a strange bittersweet tension of wanting to be somewhat better, then the balance of this book may well ease that tension.

First of all, may I repeat at the outset that it demands a certain degree of intellectual fortitude from most of us to admit we need someone or something bigger than ourselves in life. We are generally so fully preoccupied with *I* and *me* as being the most important person in all the world that we cannot conceive of anyone else usurping this position in our life. Unfortunately it is not until the stresses and storms of life have just about wrecked us that we decide to turn elsewhere for help or tranquility.

Many people assume that there is no God, or that if there is one, He is so remote and far removed from life that He simply does not count. Others have a rather detached view of Him as a benevolent being who occasionally enters their affairs. They hope that by an occasional visit to a church He will be placated to the point where perhaps He will do them a good turn if they get in a tight spot.

For all such people the things of the Spirit are on the very perimeter of life. They are relatively unimportant. They can be taken or left at will. They have virtually no bearing whatever on personal behavior. People who think this way have attempted to reduce spiritual concepts to the common ground of reason. They look on all spiritual values and relationships very lightly. Because of this they never dream that those same spiritual ideas might well prove to hold the very inner secret to life itself.

It takes some real courage to pocket our intellectual pride, face ourselves for what we are, and admit honestly that we need someone greater than ourselves to move into our lives and manage our affairs. It takes even greater courage to admit to ourselves that we need to be made over from the inside out.

I am not here writing about just theoretical or theological hypotheses. From grievous, personal, firsthand experience I know what agony of soul and anguish of heart are the lot of a man or woman far from God. Or, put in a different way, I have known the emptiness, the frustration, the pointlessness of a life which outwardly may have appeared successful but inwardly was empty and meaningless. I know the tension of trying to live my own life in my own way, while keeping God at arm's length only as a nodding acquaintance.

By the time I was into my early forties I had achieved every ambition I ever set myself in life. I had a beautiful wife, lovely children, a fine home, an excellent income, many friends, an international reputation in several fields, and a memory packed full of adventures from around the world. But inside I was hollow and empty and unfulfilled. I knew I was not the man I ought to be and I ached with a deep inner ache for something better.

Oh, I knew all about Christianity. I knew all about the church. I knew all about the historical Jesus. I was even fairly well acquainted with the theological Jesus. But I really and truly did not know God. He was not real. He was not alive. He was not active in my affairs. He was not at the center of my considerations or my deliberations. He did not control my conduct. He was not important to me. Deep down inside

I wanted Him to be, but I did not know how to accomplish this. It was like being hungry and thirsty yet finding no way to satisfy that hunger or appease that awful thirst. How could I tame this inner tension?

Then one day I read a very simple statement from Jesus' famous and well-known Sermon on the Mount. In it He said unequivocally, "Blessed are they which do hunger and thirst after righteousness, for they shall be filled!" (Matthew 5:6).

This was a categorical statement. There were no special conditions attached to it. There were no strings to it. It was not a question of reason, or logic, or thought. It was simply a straightforward case of accepting what had been said. And that is just what I did. There was nothing more involved than my complete inner accord.

It was as if I reiterated silently, "Oh God, you have declared through your Son, Jesus Christ, that if I hunger and thirst after righteousness I shall be filled. Here I am, expecting it to happen."

And it did.

God did just that. He came. His Spirit penetrated my spirit. There was a simple, quiet, serene awareness that the living Christ had come into my life by His Spirit.

There was no emotional upheaval. There was no disquieting disturbance. It was an encounter between my spirit and the Spirit of God Himself. I was standing alone at the time on a high cliff overlooking a river that wound out across the plains from the Rockies. In a sense it was as though the Spirit of God coming from the very heart of God flowed into my being in the same way that the river at my feet flowed into the empty valley before me from the snow-mantled mountains.

How had it happened?

By faith.

Faith is beyond reason. It is outside logic. It is the response of a man's spirit to the Spirit and person of God.

The greatest obstacle to the functioning of faith is intellectual pride. Its greatest incentive is humility.

Now, as I have said earlier in the book, no one is either

very keen or really able to humble himself. But circumstances and events in life have a way of humbling most of us at one time or other. And when they do we can be deeply grateful if they turn us to God.

But over and beyond all of this I do believe that reason and logic can help us to prepare our own inner hearts for faith. Surely most of us can see that life is far too complex and the world we live in too complicated for us to cope with all its difficulties alone. There is, if we are really honest about it, a need we sense to have someone greater than ourselves to whom we can turn for courage and wisdom beyond our own ability.

Just admitting this to be the case can set the proper stage for spiritual awareness. The Scriptures are very clear in emphasizing that God is pleased to enter a humble human heart by His Spirit. He actually delights to do this. But by the same measure the Scriptures are likewise very emphatic in pointing out that God actually resists and rejects those who are proud and haughty.

When in humility we approach Him in faith, it is amazing how He responds. He loves to meet us. Our faith in Him delights Him no end. We are actually told, "Without faith it is impossible to please God" (Hebrews 11:6).

It is by faith that we know God exists. It is by faith that we sense the presence of His Spirit in communication with our spirits. It is by faith that we become acquainted with the living person Jesus Christ. It is by faith that we invite Him to enter our lives as a friend, a savior, and eventually as our manager.

In all of this there is a gradual but nonetheless very real shift of interest in our affairs from a self-centered *I* or *me* to another—*He*—the living God. And as this relationship ripens we find it maturing into seeing ourselves no longer as solitary souls but as members of a family, the family of God.

This is part of the fascinating and wondrous work done by the Spirit of God Himself within my spirit. It is He who makes me keenly aware that I have become a child of God. It is He who makes me feel very much accepted by God as my

Father. It is He who brings home to me again and again the calm, quiet assurance that because I am His child and He is my Father, all of my activities, welfare, and life are very much His immediate concern.

Within such a real and vital personal relationship many of the problems and the complexities in life lose their fear. There is a sense of reassuring security which enfolds me, and I become a relaxed and serene sort of person. "God has not given us the spirit of fear; but of power and of love and of a sound mind" (II Timothy 1:7).

To live in this atmosphere, with this attitude of mind, is not to have found an escape hatch through which one ducks to avoid the harsh realities of living. Quite the contrary. It is to face positively all the futilities and frustrations and fears with a calm, quiet spirit free of tension and undue anxiety.

Better still, this firsthand acquaintance between a person and the living God adds great significance and special meaning to all one's movements. There is a new awareness that life is much more than just a haphazard sequence of random events. There is a growing consciousness that even the trivial details do have import and consequence, not only for me as a child of God, but also for all others whom my life and influence touch.

I know of nothing else in all the world which gives such tremendous dignity to living. I know of nothing else which so constrains me to live life on a level above the common crowd. I know of nothing else which infuses such an aura of adventure and excitement into living as the concept that God my Father cares very deeply what I do and how I do it. This idea lifts me from the level of living as I like—just any old way—to living with great purpose and enormous depth.

In this discussion I am deliberately avoiding the scriptural or theological language used in the Bible to portray this pattern of life. But to give the reader an inkling of how far Scripture goes in this direction, I would point out that there are passages which refer to God's children as "ambassadors," as "priests," as "heirs" of God and "joint heirs with Christ," even as "kings."

Now all of this is both possible and practical through faith, this faith having as its object God Himself, and His own declarations of commitment to us. It is true to say He does not ask us to do anything more than He Himself is prepared to match. He does not invite us to commit ourselves to Him without in turn committing Himself to us. Knowing God in an intimate way is very much a two-way proposition. The instant we respond by faith in any way either to Him or His statements, He reciprocates. The net result is a most cordial cooperative relationship.

Put in another way, God Himself is faithful to Himself; He is faithful to His commitments; He is faithful to His friends; He is faithful to His children. The person who makes this firsthand discovery moves into a marvelous area of carefree living. This is perhaps the most important statement made in this entire book. There is absolutely nothing else which can guarantee quiet repose and happy confidence in life—only the personal, firsthand knowledge that comes from experiencing the faithfulness of God.

All through our careers we may have found other human beings unreliable. We may have felt people were fickle and unpredictable. We may have been let down, double-crossed, misunderstood, and even hated without cause. All of life, its events and its supposed realities, may have mocked us. We may have feared to put reliance on anything or anyone. But anyone who has really and truly had a firsthand encounter with God will know from experience that He is utterly reliable, unchanging, and ever faithful.

No doubt there will be some who read this and say, "Oh, that's all very well for those who have faith, but what about the rest of us who haven't got this faith? How does one get it? Or if one has a wee bit, how can it be increased or strengthened?

There are several fairly simple answers to these questions.

First of all it needs to be understood that everyone has a chance to demonstrate or exercise faith. For faith is actually an act of my will in response to God. If I react or respond positively when He comes to me, there is cooperation on my part. This is positive faith or, as Scripture calls it, "the faith of obedience."

If, on the other hand, I react negatively, I reject His overtures deliberately. I refuse to cooperate; I will not believe in what I have seen, heard, or know of God—no matter how He tries to make contact with me.

It will be recalled that in the previous chapter I said God could be known through nature, through other people's godly lives, through what had been written or spoken of Him, and through His Son Christ Jesus.

The Spirit of God may use any one of these four ways to approach us. If we spurn and reject His approach, of course He can do no more. It takes two to make a mutual contact. He may come again and again, but my refusal to respond demonstrates not only the deliberate exercise of my will but also lack of faith.

If, on the other hand, an individual does react positively, if there is a cooperative response, this is faith in action, otherwise known as the faith of obedience, which is such a thrill to God.

Assuming now that one has exercised even just a faint glimmer of faith, how can it be increased? The most simple way is to be humble enough to acknowledge openly we have little faith and ask God pointblank to give us the fortitude to act in faith. The cry of the distressed soul who came to Christ and pleaded, "Lord, I believe, help thou mine unbelief!" is a classic example of honesty which was immediately honored and vindicated.

We are given to understand clearly that faith is one of the gifts which God's Spirit enjoys bringing to hungry hearts. So if there is an obvious lack of simple faith, just ask for it. He will be delighted to grant the request.

There are a few commonly held misunderstandings about faith. There is the idea abroad that the success or failure of one's acquaintance with and confidence in God depends on the degree of faith one has. It is wrongly assumed that if there is great, strong faith, fantastic results will occur. If faith is weak, then little will happen. Jesus in His comparison of faith to a grain of mustard seed held this whole concept up to ridicule.

The important thing to remember about faith is that it is the object upon which it is centered that validates it, not the inherent strength or weakness of the faith itself. If faith, no matter how weak, responds to and resides in God and in His Son Christ Jesus, it becomes strong, virile, unshakable. If, on the other hand, our faith, even though enormous, is centered in circumstances or changing human nature, then it is likely to be broken, crushed, and rendered of no avail simply because it is lodged in something unreliable.

Perhaps a simple illustration will help the reader to grasp this cardinal concept. I hope ardently it may also encourage someone to put his confidence in God.

Let us suppose a young lady falls in love with a handsome young man who appears to have excellent qualities. She responds to his advances. She has enormous faith in him. She accepts his proposal. They are married and so enter a mutual life of commitment. In due course he proves to be unfaithful. Her heart is shattered. Her home is broken. Her dreams are dashed. It is doubtful indeed if ever again she can have a particle of faith in any man.

But by and by she meets another gentleman. Again something about his approach attracts her. She has to muster all her resources to trust him. Her faith in him is very feeble, very flickering. Finally she decides to give marriage another try. But she is not at all sure. Her man this time turns out to be utterly reliable. She has a happy heart. Her home is a joy. Her fondest dreams are fulfilled.

What has made the difference? Is it her great faith or little faith? Neither. The degree of her faith had nothing to do with it.

The difference was made by the caliber of the person in whom her faith resided. It was the character of the second man that made her faith a glorious joy.

And so it is with our faith in God. It does not depend on either its own inherent strength or its weakness. It depends, rather, entirely on the character and person of God Himself.

Because God is who He is and has such an impeccable character we may be utterly sure our confidence in Him, our faith in Him, will never be betrayed. What a tonic for tension!

17

The Character of Christ

It was Jesus Christ Himself who made the unequivocal statement, "He that has seen me hath seen the Father" (John 14:9). All through His years of public appeal and teaching Jesus repeatedly emphasized this point. He made it abundantly clear that He and His Father were one, that He was doing exactly what His Father would do, that He so lived in God and God His Father so lived in Him that they were in fact one and the same person.

This, then, being the case, it is obvious that to understand and appreciate the character of God, we must of necessity look at the character of Christ. To see the one is to see the other.

One of the gigantic achievements accomplished during the few short years of Christ's life was the precise portrayal given to us of God Himself. Sometimes I feel we miss this point completely. Paul makes much of it. He declares dramatically in Colossians 1:15, "Now Christ is the visible expression of the invisible God" (J. B. Phillips).

In view of the above facts we should not hesitate, then, to

take a long, hard look at the life of our Lord. He is the one in whom we are putting our confidence. He is the one who must of necessity validate our faith. He is the one who ultimately vindicates the reliance invested in Him. He is the one who makes our relationship in a spiritual dimension both real and workable. He is the one who makes genuine Christianity a superior and serene way of life.

In essence it is Christ Himself who makes our Christian faith unique among the world's many religions, creeds, philosophies, and teachings. Jesus, the Christ, was not a mere man; He was not just another "good" man; He was not just another prophet in the long succession of prophets; He was not just a moralizer with a higher code of ethics; He was not just another great thinker; He was not just a mighty philosopher of unusual perception; He was not just a new teacher of radical or revolutionary ideals.

The truth is that He was all of these and much more. He was God in human guise. He was God garbed in human flesh, expressing Himself through human personality. In so doing He gave us a precise portrayal of God's character. In the very nature of things He could not do otherwise. He had to be true to Himself, and He was.

This brings us to the first concept of His character that arouses our attention and admiration. He was not only utterly truthful but He was truth. This is a formidable fact for us to face.

The vast majority of our problems in human relations stem from the simple fact that people are not true. People from childhood are drilled in duplicity. It is not that they deliberately set out to be scoundrels, but rather that they tend to twist, distort, and manipulate matters in such a way as to always protect themselves. All of us are caught up in the vicious struggle of self-preservation. Therefore something must be sacrificed to insure our survival, and more often than not it is truth which is made the victim.

Basically this explains our human sense of insecurity. Again and again through life we hear the common comment, "I just cannot trust him!" This lack of trust that is so apparent between people lies at the heart of much human tension. The fact that we find even friends unreliable tends to fill us with apprehension. Men and women discover through the most bitter and burning experiences that even members of their own families may prove false. They simply are not true to one another. Or, put another way, there is no truth in their statements nor in their behavior.

I am keenly aware that some still contend that the majority of human beings are basically honest. This contention simply is not so. If it were, there would be no need for laws or codes of human conduct to control society.

The enormous lengths taken in almost every area of life for self-protection stand as undeniable evidence that we human beings really don't trust each other. We put confidence in one another only to the degree that our self-interests are safeguarded and preserved by all sorts of complex social rules and regulations. These are laid down in infinite detail amid masses of lengthy laws.

In contrast to all this Christ stands among men and declares, "I am truth." In Him there was not a particle of hypocrisy. He had no false front, no duplicity, no double talk. It was this characteristic of utter truthfulness which so enraged the hypocritical Pharisees and ecclesiastical intelligentsia of His day.

As a matter of fact it is His utter honesty, His absolute veracity, which all through history has alienated dishonest and insincere people. The double-dealers and cunning contrivers have always tried to belittle, deny, and even destroy the truth expressed in the character of Christ. They have done this simply because He made them so uncomfortable. Little wonder they crucified Jesus; no less wonder He is still scorned.

But for the man or woman who wants security, who seeks serenity, who is searching for someone to really trust, He still stands waiting quietly. He is no different now than He was when He tramped over the bare, brown, sun-baked hills of Palestine. Whenever a soul, soured and scarred by betrayed trust in other people, turns to Him, it finds truth and integrity and utter honesty.

We see this drama depicted over and over in the day-to-day incidents of His life. Men and women whose lives were nightmares of agony, whose hearts had been broken by betrayed love, whose tensions and anxieties were destroying their most cherished relationships, came to Christ and found fresh hope and new life. What is more, they found rest for the simple reason they had found someone on whom they could rely.

We can well understand what an amazing experience it must have been for ordinary human beings to meet the Christ, who was totally truthful and absolutely honest. It was akin to stumbling on an oasis with clear bubbling springs of truth amid the dreadful desolation of a vast desert of dishonesty.

Is it any wonder that poor prostitutes, crude fishermen, ordinary children, and cunning tax collectors were captivated by Christ and came to consider Him their closest friend? But beyond all this, they learned to love Him dearly.

What happened then still happens today. When any person is prepared to come to Christ in open, honest humility, without pretense or sham, he at once finds a friend. There is an immediate response from our own inner spirit to the Spirit of truth apparent in the person of Jesus Christ. There is an attraction which is generated through our finding someone worthy of our utmost confidence and trust. There is nothing in life so calculated to relieve tension and strain as knowing there is a friend available to whom we can turn in every situation.

Best of all are the quiet assurance and very comforting knowledge that Christ never does betray the confidence we put in Him. He never does let us down. He never does double-cross us. He never plays us false.

Next to the truthfulness and utter integrity of Christ, perhaps His most important characteristic is His strength. This may seem a strange thing to say, for far too often He has been depicted as rather a frail figure. Well-intentioned but grossly misleading descriptions of Him such as "gentle Jesus, meek and mild" have done God an enormous disservice.

Not for a moment do I deny that Christ was one of the world's truly great gentlemen. Nor do I wish to detract in any way from His amazing humility and utter graciousness. But He was no milquetoast. Nor was He a shaky-kneed weakling. Nor did He ever cringe or cower in the presence of terrible pressures put upon Him. Rather He stands as a great mountain of divine manhood completely overshadowing and overtowering both His contemporaries and all subsequent geniuses.

Actually one of the terrible injustices the Christian church has done to Christ's character is its attempt to confine Him to a merely human concept. Too often He is portrayed as a pathetic babe in arms, an emaciated, white-faced, feeble man, a broken corpse on Calvary's cross, or even worse, a plaster-cast character with a halo around His head.

Many of these impressions of the person of Christ have come down to us through the centuries. They have been conveyed to us in unrealistic art, rather insipid writings, distorted pageantry, and the peculiar patterns of human thought whereby we attempt to reduce the Lord of the Universe to the level of our own frail flesh.

It is highly important, therefore, for us to take another look at Jesus Christ in the context of His own behavior among us. There is little value in merely stating that being God, He is all-powerful, all-wise, and so on. Before we can believe this we must see for ourselves He could really live life in the rough-and-tumble world of men and be in complete control of every situation He encountered.

After all we must remind ourselves that He said not only, "I am the truth," but also, "I am the way, and the truth, and the life." In other words, He was demonstrating how to live life in a way which embodied enormous dignity, strength, and quiet assurance.

Those of us who think hard and deeply about the difficulties of society have long since realized that one of its major problems is the basic insecurity of people. As time goes on, men and women seem less and less able to cope with the complexities of their own society. There is an uneasy feeling that things are out of control and one can do very little about it.

No one seems to have the answers, and if a solution is found for one problem, a dozen new ones spring up in its place.

Against such a bizarre and bewildering background it comes as a tremendous tonic and inspiration for us to discover someone who has the answers. It is an enormous uplift to find in Christ a character of such unusual strength that He is able to cope readily with every exigency of life. What is even more remarkable, we find here a person whose character is of such force and dynamic power that He not only copes with but actually controls and directs all events.

Always, always, we must think of Christ and see Him as the "one in control," the "one in charge," the "one in command." He was not a victim of circumstances. He was not a pawn on the chessboard of life, pushed about and manipulated at will.

From His boyhood to His ascension we stand in awe at the strong, quiet, superior way in which Christ moved through life. In the temple at the age of twelve He was already able to hold the attention of much older men steeped in the Scriptures of His people. In the carpenter's shop He was the craftsman with skill enough to earn an adequate livelihood for His widowed mother and younger siblings. In fact by the time He was thirty He must have set aside sufficient savings to provide for His family's welfare while He went away on His public ministry.

We see Him, strong in body, toughened by toil, browned by the sun, starting off towards the Jordan to be publicly baptized by John the Baptist. At once He is recognized by that great mystic as a man apart, one whose shoe latchets the Baptist is unworthy to unfasten. Here is a giant among His contemporaries, and John makes no bones about it.

Instinctively, rugged young men are attracted to Jesus Christ. The majority of His followers are in their late teens or early twenties. They are attracted by the strength, the courage, the purpose of this person. He epitomizes their highest aspirations. Willingly they turn away from their assorted trades to tramp the endless sun-scorched miles with Him.

For nearly three years the hearty band will share their

meals and beds beneath open skies. It takes stamina and vigor and vitality to live like this, where each soon discovers all the strengths and weaknesses of his fellows. Here there can be no sham, no false front, no coverup. And Christ lived this way, calling His companions "friends," despite all the times they disappointed Him.

We see Christ alone in the desert, dealing with the devil. We see Him handle that crafty character with such consummate skill and strength that the "old snake" is soon on the run.

We see Him in the storms that blow up with such frequency on the Lake of Galilee. He but speaks a word and the winds die, the waves subside. Here is one totally in control of even the basic physical elements, just as He is utterly in control of spiritual powers.

This Christ could turn water to wine, just as He could turn sinning men and women into saints. He could take a boy's small buns and bless them to feed thousands of famished people. In the same way He could take a handful of spiritual food and break it down to simple truth able to satisfy a thousand hungry hearts.

It takes strength of spirit, toughness of mind, and immense moral insight to achieve these results. It doesn't just happen. It happens only when the basic ingredients for achieving miracles are held in the control of one with unusual capacities. And never has a character of comparable stature stepped upon the world scene. Like all great geniuses, He achieved what He did without fanfare or show.

We find Him confronted with disease, death, and even decay of human flesh. None of these deter Him. He does not try to avoid them or evade the demands they put upon Him. Instead He deals with them deftly and convincingly. The blind see; the deaf hear; the dumb speak; the lepers are cured; the lame walk; the dead are raised; the forces of decomposition are reversed.

This was not mass hypnotism. It was not black magic. It was not witchcraft or mind over matter. It was the strength of one in harmony with His Father, simply demonstrating His enormous power on behalf of others.

We see Jesus Christ approaching Calvary. We see Him deliberately choose to die, the just one in place of the guilty ones. We see Him not as a martyr but as a quiet monarch deciding His own end. Despite the trumped-up charges, despite the kangaroo court, despite the scheming and knavery of His accusers, we see this strong one emerge from the ordeal unscathed and unsullied. Always He is in charge of events.

Even on the cross, amid appalling agony, He is able to grant pardon to His accusers and look with love upon His mother, commending her to another's care. It takes a giant of a character to so conduct oneself, and Christ was just that.

At last we see Him triumph over death. We see Him shatter the shackles of the grave. We see Him ascend to be seated in honor and splendor and might at His Father's right hand. None other ever deserved such exaltation. None other has ever demonstrated such fortitude and strength of character to attain it.

So I say that it is no small thing to have our confidence in Christ, the living Lord. To know that we have someone of this caliber to whom we may entrust ourselves in every situation is to have found one of the great secrets to serene living.

Here is one always in control. Here is one able to meet any exigency in life. Here is one with the answers to every dilemma.

What a friend to find! What a companion in whom we may put our confidence. What a one to take control of our affairs and our lives—if we will let Him.

This leads us to consider the next amazing aspect of Christ's character—namely, His approachability. Notwithstanding His utter truthfulness and His magnificent strength, there is something immensely warm and endearing about Christ. He is not a far-off God ensconced somewhere in the distant skies. Nor is He a dusty, ancient historical character obscured in the haze of antiquity. Nor is He a stern, august adjudicator standing afar in dour judgment. Nor is He merely a mysterious mystic.

He is Jesus, the Christ, with the common touch for common men. He is the suffering Savior who was a man of sorrows and acquainted with grief—our sort of grief. He did not come to condemn the world but to redeem it; He did not come to judge us but to lift us up. His main mission was to bind up the brokenhearted, to set free captives, to comfort all that mourn, to give beauty in place of ashes and the oil of joy and garment of praise in place of heavy spirits.

Is it any marvel men and women come to Him? Is it any wonder that people learn to love Him so dearly?

18

The Love of God

In one way it would have been better to entitle this chapter "The God of Love." I say this because in contemplating the character of God, as seen in Christ, we are immediately impressed by His unparalleled love.

If by chance anyone thinks of God apart from and outside of the context of love, then it is fairly safe to say he really does not know Him. For, of all God's attributes, none is so apparent as His love. It completely overshadows all of the integrity, strength, humility, and approachability discussed in the previous chapter. Basically it was the love in Christ's life which drew men and women to Him. It was His completely open selflessness which made such an enormous impact on the people of His time.

Before we can understand this we must grasp the true significance of God's love. We must understand and appreciate what sort of love it is. We cannot equate it with the types of so-called love which are commonly referred to in our human language, especially in the English idiom.

Throughout the Scriptures reference is made to three kinds

of love. The first I shall mention is that of a purely physical nature. It is the mutual response between male and female. It is what the modern world and modern men and women think of immediately when the word *love* is mentioned. Unfortunately it has been reduced to little more than mere sex. Yet in Scripture it is still a sublime relationship between two people, each of whom has committed himself completely to the other. It is part of God's profound planning for parenthood, and in its proper setting provides human beings with an enormous sense of security and serenity within the sanctuary of a home.

The second sort of love dealt with in Scripture is commonly referred to as filial love. It is the deep devotion and affection which can grow between brothers and sisters, parents and children, mutual friends, members of the same community, or even men and women caught up in a common cause; for example, in battle, servicemen will actually lay down their lives for their mates, or men engaged in research or exploration or adventure will readily risk themselves for the welfare of their companions.

This love is lodged in the realm of our minds and emotions. It is born through close and continuous contact of men and women in any given situation. It may commence with the most casual acquaintance, grow into mutual respect or admiration, and finally flower in the full-blown reality of an abiding and enduring affection.

The third kind of love spoken of in Scripture is the love of God. It is love in its deepest and most profound spiritual sense. This is a sort of love which few people know much about. It is a love totally transcending the other two.

This love is, for want of a better definition, absolute selflessness. It is the spirit of putting others' interests always ahead of one's own. It is the inner attitude of laying oneself out at any cost for others, even one's enemies. Actually it implies giving up one's own rights and prerogatives in order to be completely available to others. In short, it is death to self.

It is precisely at this point where we find that this love is essential to a life free from tension and anxiety. I say this simply because anyone who experiences it in a personal contact with Christ is suddenly set free from the anxieties attached to ordinary human love at its lower levels.

In the very nature of things we soon discover in life that in order to be loved either in a physical or filial dimension we must show ourselves lovable. Somehow we have to demonstrate to others that we are worth loving. We have to prove that we are worthy of their love. And, sad to say, in most cases, the moment we fail to do this we discover that we are being cut off. The very fact that we may fail to live up to the expectations of others may induce them to lose interest in us; their confidence is shaken; they may feel a bit betrayed and so their love to us dries up.

This explains why families break up. It explains why husbands and wives separate. It explains why brothers and sisters or parents and children may become deeply alienated and antagonistic. It explains why the best of friends may become the worst of enemies. It explains why in society as a whole there is the endless fret over offending others. It explains why so many people live under constant tension trying to hold their homes together. It explains the feverish fear of losing friends and making enemies.

Now, amazing as it may sound, and incredible as it may seem, there is none of this in the love of God. The simple truth is that His love for me does not in any way depend on my worthiness of it. In other words, I do not have to merit His love. I do not, so to speak, have to earn His love.

Scripture repeats this theme again and again. For example, in that most poignant of all the stories told by Jesus, the account of the prodigal son, we see clearly portrayed for us what the love of God is like. In fact Christ used this parable to convey concisely what is meant by God's love.

Here was a young man who deliberately chose to squander his father's hard-won earnings. He was a strong-willed, selfish young upstart who set out to live it up, no matter what the consequences. Not only did he heap shame upon himself but he also dragged his father's reputation into disgrace. More than that he knowingly grieved the dear old man and broke his heart with anxiety.

In the normal course of events, especially in the Middle East, such a son would have been long since disowned. He would have been disinherited. He would have been banished forever from the home.

But in one of the most poignant word pictures ever painted, Christ shows the father's reaction when his prodigal son turns toward home. He runs to him. He embraces him. He kisses him. He brushes aside his protestations of unworthiness. He puts a new, clean cloak around him, fresh shoes on his feet, a ring on his finger. The feast is prepared. This is the love of God.

No doubt the dear old man had died a thousand deaths after his son's departure. Without question he had been humiliated into the dust by the damaging reports that came back to him of his son's conduct. Certainly his hair must have turned gray and his eyes red with weeping as he wondered what would become of his son.

Yet his attitude of devotion, affection, and utter selflessness never altered. It mattered not what happened to himself as long as his son could be restored and redeemed and remade. His care and concern for this one's welfare never abated.

This is the love of God.

This is utter selflessness.

This is total self-sacrifice.

Little marvel, then, that men and women who have encountered this sort of love are set free from fear. For the first time in life they have found a love so great, so magnanimous, so generous it does not depend on their behavior or their worthiness. Rather, it is expressed simply because it is in fact a very part of God Himself. It is His own inherent character. For as John the beloved apostle wrote so emphatically, *"God is love."*

The truly thrilling and wonderful release that attends an encounter with Christ is something which has to be experienced before it can be fully appreciated. For the first time one is set free from the fear and worry of not being worthy, of not being lovable, of not deserving such love. Instead there comes the calm, quiet delight of knowing I am loved simply because Christ loves me, God loves me!

Trying to put this on paper in mere human language is an almost impossible endeavor. I am here dealing with a subject of such enormous spiritual significance that it will scarcely submit to such simple treatment as I have given it. Still the fact remains that for those few who have found the love of God, life is never quite the same again.

Once this love has swept into their spirits it replaces the old stagnant hates, fears, worries, prejudices, and fret with its own pure stream. Attitudes alter. We begin to see others in a new light and in a new way. Our entire outlook on others changes. We find the statement made by Paul in II Timothy 1:7 to be an absolute reality, "For God hath not given us a spirit of fear, but of love and of power and of a sound [disciplined] mind."

Or to put it as John does, "We love, because he first loved us" (I John 4:19). And to our own astonishment we find that our love both to God Himself and to others is intensified. Perhaps previously we may not have so much as given God more than a casual passing thought. Suddenly, now, Christ becomes to us the dearest friend. We actually take delight in living to please Him. His incredible love extended to us in spite of our unworthiness elicits an enthusiastic and spontaneous response from us so now we do endeavor deliberately to live worthy of such a one.

Likewise in our relationship with others. No longer do we stand in judgment of their every action and attitude. Instead, broken and humbled by the love of God given to us, we turn to our fellow human beings and extend the same compassion to them.

The whole question of forgiveness follows the same lines. It has amazed me to discover how many people live under tension because of unforgiven issues in their lives. Either they themselves feel unforgiven or they hold grudges and grievances against others, refusing to grant forgiveness for some wrong or injury they may have suffered. How often we hear the bitter remark, "I will never forgive them for it," or, "I will never forgive myself for behaving in the way I did."

Now it is quite impossible for anyone to have such an attitude and experience serenity. A lack of forgiveness generates tensions and anxieties at the very deepest levels of human experience. Nothing can be more insidious than the inner turmoil of an unforgiving or unforgiven spirit.

We humans are past masters at the art of self-deception. All too often we simply assume rather naively that time will take care of such tensions. We try to shrug them off. We attempt to dismiss them from our lives or bury them in forgetfulness. But unfortunately if we can't forgive, we can't forget. So the old animosity or alienation rankles deep within our spirits like a worm boring through a beautiful fruit. Unless, ultimately, the matter is resolved, the entire life can be blighted.

In our relationship to God most of us stagger along through life with the same sort of apprehensions. We are quite sure our conduct does not meet with His approval. We sense a certain degree of guilt because of our misdeeds. In our better moments we wish we could do better. But on the whole we really wonder if we can be forgiven our faults and failings.

All of this is very disconcerting. Certainly it cannot contribute to a quiet and contented spirit. But at the same time few people know how their dilemma can be resolved.

I recall vividly an experience of this kind with a dear lady who suffered from Parkinson's disease. She had regularly attended church. But it was quite obvious that just going to services and listening to sermons had not solved the inner tensions which tormented her. Most of her difficulties revolved around the question of forgiveness.

One morning, sitting quietly beside me on the sofa in her living room, she began to unburden herself to me. "Do you really think, Mr. Keller," she said, looking deep into my eyes, "that God can really forgive me for all my past?" She was not an emotional woman. Her eyes were hard and piercing and very searching as she asked the stabbing question.

Instead of answering her from my own background I asked her to turn to the story of the prodigal boy. Together we read through Luke 15:11-20. When we read that the lad's father saw him coming, had compassion, and ran to embrace him, I turned and said, "You see, the father never stopped loving him. He *was* forgiven before he ever got back!" There was a pause between us of several moments' silence.

She turned to me and said softly, "You mean God, my Father, has already forgiven me?"

"Yes," I replied gently, "You are forgiven! All you have to do is accept the forgiveness."

She suddenly snatched up a box of Kleenex and the tissues tumbled out one after another as she tried to stanch the stream of tears that flooded from her eyes.

"Don't feel bad, Mr. Keller!" she exclaimed. "They are tears of pure joy—pure joy. I have been forgiven. I *am* forgiven!"

Such is the liberation of a spirit set free from the tormenting tensions of guilt, self-accusation, and feeling unforgiven. And may I add, only the man or woman who knows such release is in turn able to extend complete and wholehearted forgiveness to fellow human beings.

On the surface this may all seem quite simple. And in a sense it is. God, in Christ, has been good enough to make our contacts and relationship with Him simple and uncomplicated, so much so that even a small child or the most untutored savage can come. Still this does not detract from the drastic and deeply profound measures taken by God Himself, in love, to make this possible.

I say this lest the reader assume that God is so soft and sentimental that He merely overlooks our faults and more or less winks at our misconduct.

Just the opposite is so. Being who He is, not only loving and merciful and forgiving, but also strong, honest, just, and utterly righteous, He cannot tolerate our misdeeds. Most of us in our more somber moments will admit to ourselves, if not to others, that we are not deserving of His love. We know instinctively that we ought to suffer the penalty for our own perverseness. We sense a real wretchedness in the presence of Christ's own impeccable character. Yet wonder of wonders,

He does not demand or insist on retribution for our misconduct. *Why?*

Because He Himself bore the penalty for our faults and failures and unforgiving spirits at Calvary. It was He who suffered in my stead. This is essentially the significance of the cross.

It is surprising how many people miss this point completely. Somehow they seem to insist all through life on trying to atone for their own misbehavior. Such an attitude keeps them under constant stress. They are always afraid that they might not be able to quite make it to heaven. They are anxious and worried lest their bad behavior outweigh their charitable deeds. So they stagger through life carrying a depressing load of anxiety. These strains and stresses are not figments of their imagination; they are very real tensions which can work havoc with both their mental and physical well-being.

But, on the other hand, when we come to Christ, or, if you wish, come home to our heavenly Father in simplicity, these tensions are immediately tamed. First we suddenly see that we are in fact loved by God our Father despite our misdeeds. Then we discover that we are forgiven despite all the damage we have done, and finally it dawns upon us that He is the one who has borne the cost of our misconduct at His own expense on Calvary.

Really all that is required is for me to accept these facts. The moment I do, a tremendous sense of emancipation sweeps through my spirit. I am set free! All the old gnawing guilt, anxieties, and tensions are gone. And at last it is possible to relax and feel at home with God, for in fact that is exactly what has happened. I have come home to my heavenly Father.

Once this happens to us, and we know the intoxicating delight of having been set free, suddenly our attitude to others alters. It is quite impossible for anyone who has sensed his own forgiveness by God to go out and harbor grudges against another person. This is perhaps a shocking statement to make. It needs to be made with emphasis. For the degree to which I sense and appreciate God's forgiveness to me in very large measure determines how willing I am to forgive others. By the same measurement, the depth to which I feel and perceive the love of God my Father for me decides exactly how much compassion and concern I can bear towards others.

There is no substitute for love and forgiveness and compassionate human understanding to ease friction and reduce the strains and stresses which arise between human beings. And when I pause to reflect that God, who knows the worst about me, is still willing to love, forgive, and cherish me, then there is a strong stimulus for me to extend the same treatment to others.

As I grow to be an older man and look back down the long trail of my life, perhaps the most poignant thought which comes to me again and again is the unrelenting love of God to me and His unlimited forgiveness despite all my failures. Nothing so warms my heart towards Him. Nothing so stimulates my spirit with hope and zest. And may I add, nothing else so induces me to extend a measure of compassion, love, and forgiveness to my fellows on the tough trail of life. It helps ease the strain on all of us.

I wish to point out and emphasize that this magnanimous attitude towards others represents no special merit, no particular good on my part. It does not even have its origin with me. Rather it is the result of the inflow of God's Spirit and life into my life. It is the passing on to others of the love, compassion, forgiveness, and sympathetic understanding extended to me by God.

This in itself produces both in me and in others a relaxed sense of goodwill. It banishes the old behavior patterns of bitterness, hate, and tension that torment us. Added to all this is a lighthearted freedom from the old nagging fears that taunt those who have never felt forgiven or are unable to forgive. Life becomes a cheerful adventure instead of a drab ordeal because one can be utterly open, honest, and fully available to others.

After all, this is precisely what God Himself has done for us in Christ at Calvary and what Christ now continues to do as the living, exalted Lord. He is always laying Himself out for us. He is always making Himself available to us by His own gracious Spirit. He is ever coming to us in heartwarming affection. He is ever reassuring us of His love, His concern, His forgiveness, His interest in our welfare.

All of this is part and parcel of the love of God. Such love is so utterly foreign to so many that they can scarcely believe it to be true. This is complete selflessness and self-sacrifice in contradistinction to our usual human selfishness. Wherever it touches our lives and enters our hearts, it begins its own wondrous work of transformation.

19

*Belonging to
God's Family*

From our earliest years all of us instinctively crave to belong to a group. We yearn to be a part of a social community. Because of our very makeup, most of us are most comfortable, most at ease, most relaxed in the company of others who accept us as one of their own.

We find, for example, that tiny tots become very uneasy and tense the moment they are cut off from the comfort and companionship of Mother and Dad. Every growing child finds a certain degree of confidence and assurance by belonging to a family. And, if by some upheaval the family is fractured and divided, its members undergo enormous stresses and strains.

It is common knowledge that young people who are exposed to the anxieties inherent in broken homes become very insecure. Somehow they seem to fear that even worse tragedies can overtake them at any time. They become suspicious of others and tend to build high walls of self-defense around themselves to protect their lives from further suffering.

Any person who at any time has been rejected by a group to which he belonged carries a certain stigma of failure and frustration. He may make repeated attempts to prove himself in order to become accepted again. It is surprising the lengths to which some will go in order to become identified with a group. This explains much teen-age behavior. And if they don't make it into the group and are spurned, we find them retreating still deeper within their own walled fortress.

These patterns of behavior persist all through life. The up-shot is that many people are under tremendous tension simply because they do not feel they have succeeded in "belonging." In a strange way thousands of otherwise normal people feel that they are really not wanted. They may have a few casual friends or acquaintances, but still they are haunted with the painful, persistent pangs of loneliness.

The number of people who live with this sort of distress grows steadily in society. It is actually a most disquieting experience to discover firsthand just how many human beings there are who actually feel unloved, unwanted, and uncared for. They are very much alone. Life is a trial. More than that, it is a dreadful bore.

There are a number of reasons why this spirit of heaviness is spreading all through Western society. The breakup of homes alienates and divides hundreds of thousands of people. Men, women, and children feel deserted, abandoned, rejected, and unwanted. The increase in urban living has brought millions into metropolitan areas where on the surface one would imagine they could never get lonely. But a great city can be the most lonely and forbidding spot on earth. There may be hundreds of human beings around you, not one of whom cares a whit what happens to you. Coupled with city life is the modern mania to be on the move. People drift hither and yon without putting down roots. They don't belong anywhere. There is the eternal difficulty of trying to make new friends and to find someone who shows an interest in you. Finally there is old age, which medical service tends to prolong.

Often the twilight years are the most tormenting simply because one's friends and family die and depart; the younger generation is frequently so preoccupied with its own affairs that younger people find little time for the aged. More than this, old age is often beset with all sorts of stress and anxiety as one's powers and ability to cope with changing events are less effective.

So the questions have to be asked, and asked in a frank, forthright manner, "Is there an antidote for this tension of loneliness? Is there some spiritual stimulant to counteract the spirit of heaviness apparent in so many lives?"

Happily I can say yes. And I can say so with great emphasis.

It will have become apparent to the reader by this time that if one has a direct and personal encounter with God by His Spirit, some basic changes will be bound to take place in life. Of these perhaps the most beautiful, and certainly the most winsome, is the growing awareness that I am part of a new community. There steals over my spirit the assurance that I have been accepted. I sense in a strangely moving way that somehow now I do belong.

Actually what has happened is that God is no longer a distant, abstract concept on the far horizon of my life. Instead He has come close in the comforting and wonderfully reassuring role of my Father.

For my part, I am no longer just a nonentity of no consequence amid the mass of humanity. Suddenly I have become a child of God, an individual in whom my heavenly Father is personally interested. Not only is He interested in me as His child, but also He is deeply concerned about every detail of my life. This means that I am now free to turn to Him about any matter that might arise, knowing that I shall get a sympathetic hearing.

Such a relationship immediately sets me free from tensions which could torment me. First of all, it is wonderful to belong to Him and know I am wanted. Secondly, it is thrilling to sense that someone is sufficiently interested in my affairs to give me sympathetic attention.

In addition to this I find in Christ, God's other Son, not only a Savior, but also a friend and brother. He Himself used these terms, so I make no apologies for doing the same. He invites me to share with Him all the events of my life.

It is this ready acceptability that makes our relationship so real and meaningful. It requires no special ritual, no ornate sanctuary, no ecclesiastical hierarchy or priesthood for me to present Him with my petitions. I simply come on the spur of the moment and tell Him all about my affairs. He enjoys knowing about my good times just as much as He wants to sympathize with my difficulties. And we do Him a distinct disservice if we dump only our troubles in His lap. After all, He wants to rejoice with me just as much as He is willing to weep with me.

I have purposely avoided using the word *prayer* up to this point in the book simply because for so many it smacks of musty churches, mournful music, and boring rituals. But basically, true prayer is simply a quiet, sincere, genuine conversation with God. It is a two-way dialogue between friends.

Of course the moment I mention prayer a good many people may feel a bit put off. After all, they assume, this is some sort of pious exercise performed almost as a painful penance by priests, preachers, and other plaster-cast recluses.

Genuine prayer is nothing of the sort. It is the heartfelt impressions of my spirit finding expression in such a way that they elicit a response from the Spirit of God. For both my heavenly Father and Christ my Savior do speak to me by the Spirit. He is the one who conveys to me in a still, small, inner voice the thoughts, impulses, and intentions of God. He does this both directly with distinct impressions upon my spirit and indirectly through outer influences such as the advice of godly friends, the trend of current circumstances, the reading of Scripture, or even the natural phenomena of the world around me.

No matter how or when a conversation is carried on within the family of God, it continually convinces and reassures me of the presence and approachability of my heavenly Father. Few relationships in life can be as heartening and inspiring as this. It is the great elixir of life. No longer do I live on the common level. I sense that I have been lifted up into a new dimension of living in which I actually walk and talk with God my Father and His Son my Brother. My earthly sojourn is not just a barren, boring existence dragged on from day to day of unbearable loneliness and pointlessness. Now it becomes a bright adventure with each new day charged with eager anticipation.

It needs to be made clear that this sort of close and intimate relationship with God does not just happen in a moment, so to speak. Just as with a human relationship, it requires time and care to cultivate this cherished family life. Too many of us turn to God only in times of trouble or grief. This is a selfish way to treat Him. If we want to be generous and give Him some joy, then surely we can be big enough to share our sanguine, happy moments with Him as well.

A fact few people realize is that it is possible to give God great joy. It is one of the ways we can demonstrate to Him that we do truly appreciate all that He does for us. It proves beyond doubt that we don't take Him for granted. Throughout Scripture, this is referred to as "praising Him." But the word *praise* is gradually changing in meaning. Nowadays when we speak of praising a person the idea that springs to mind is one of flattery or commendation. But God our Father does not want either our flattery or a pat on the back. What He really wants and deeply appreciates is our genuine gratitude.

Because of this I do not hesitate to say that the person who has learned to live in an "attitude of gratitude" for all God's benefits has found one of the great secrets to successful spiritual living. Nothing pleases God more than our deep appreciation for all that He has done and all that He is. We soon discover that just as there is great tranquility in a human family where appreciation is frequently expressed, so the same is true in the family of God. Try it and you will find your days are full of delight rather than drabness.

It is my personal conviction that faith and gratitude go hand in hand. If anything, one could say that gratitude grows out of faith. It is the expression of appreciation for confidence vindicated.

In our relationships both with God and others it is beautiful to see how gratitude generates confidence and confidence honored, in turn, produces gratitude. And when these both function harmoniously in our everyday experiences we find ourselves set free from much of the frustration and fretting that make up the fever of living.

It is a tremendous tonic for a mere mortal to know that he is in personal contact with the immortal. And when such a contact is continuous it gradually dawns upon him that he, too, is partaking of this same immortality. Put in another way, once I find myself a member of God's family, I realize that a very real rebirth has occurred. I have been remade. My attitudes alter, my outlook on life is redirected, and my entire conduct takes on a new tenor.

Probably the most significant aspect of this new relationship is an overwhelming sense of genuine gratitude to God for what has happened. Coupled with this is a keen awareness of having been set free from the old fears and anxieties. It is possible now to relax and enjoy the benefits bestowed on me without worrying about trying to earn them or merit some special favor through adhering to rigid rules.

The Scriptures, of course, state that this should be so. But few people seem to express proper gratitude. Yet when I truly realize what privileges have been bestowed on me in becoming God's child, there is bound to be enormous gratitude.

This gratitude finds expression in many ways. It is a continuous appreciation for all that Christ has achieved for me by His life, death, resurrection, and teaching. It is a genuine thankfulness for the presence and guidance of God's Spirit. It is a never-failing delight over knowing God as my Father and His knowing me as His child.

All of this gives enormous impetus to the human spirit. But it also goes far beyond just the spiritual realm. We become keenly aware that every good thing which we enjoy has had its origin with God. All the events of life take on special significance because we are aware that they are part of our

Father's plan and purpose for us, His blueprint for us.

As I live in this "attitude of gratitude," even the most ordinary things become sublime. The common world around me becomes diffused with the divine. The sunrise I watched break in crimson splendor above the purple sea this morning speaks to me of His beauty and majesty. The call of the cuckoo from a nearby tree and the flight of a tiny wren remind me of His care even for birds. The steady fall of raindrops on the window and fragrance of fresh earth tell of His faithfulness in supplying sufficient moisture for all the vegetation of grass, trees, shrubs, and flowers. The smile playing upon the contented face of my wife and the shining sparkle in her warm brown eyes are a reminder of the great joys given again and again to His children.

In all of this there comes refreshment of spirit. It is like a clear, pure stream of godly gratitude that flushes away fear and foreboding, tension and strain. And life becomes beautiful when I belong to God's family.

This does not imply that there will be no troubles in life. It does not mean that there will be no gray days, no suffering, no sorrow, no tough times. But what it does mean is that no matter what comes I am better able to cope because I am in good company and I know there is someone close at hand who is deeply concerned and cares how I am getting along. This is the precious part about belonging to God's family.

Then, too, we discover that other ordinary human beings just like ourselves have become members of this same family. We sense a common bond that binds us all together. In this fraternity there are also new strength and friendship which are refreshing to our spirits. This bond unites men and women from diverse backgrounds, races, and strata of society as no other fellowship upon earth can do.

I recall clearly one day when I was somewhat lonely on a rather remote island in the mid-Pacific. For a number of reasons a mood of melancholy had settled over my spirit so that even the loveliness of the sea and the brilliance of the sunshine could not seem to rouse me. As I strolled alone along the shore, I was approached by an elderly Japanese gentleman. He smiled politely, bowed, and engaged me in casual conversation.

After a few minutes our discussion turned to deeper subjects. Soon I found he was a gracious man with a great confidence in Christ. As brothers we shared our common love for God and His for us. In a matter of an hour my spirit was singing and soaring in gratitude for this one who had crossed my path. Such are the benefits of belonging to God's family.

20

Contented Living

One of the earmarks of any person who has come into a viable and meaningful relationship with God as his heavenly Father is an attitude of quiet contentment with life. Gone are the emptiness and frustration of a pointless existence. In its place there are purpose and meaning and direction in all one does.

The above is a fairly easy statement to make on paper. The reader may pass it over almost unnoticed. But to encounter it in actual life and to find people of whom it is true is another thing. There are, in fact, very few such fortunate people. I say this simply because of the general discontent of our age.

Despite our ever-increasing affluence, despite our shorter workweeks, despite our greater leisure, despite our increased longevity, despite our more advanced technology, despite our improved social benefits, men and women are today probably more restless, more uneasy, and more discontented than ever before. Life for most seems to be a strained state of apprehension and tension. They seem to be caught up in an ever-accelerating stream of events over which they have little or no control. They are swept along on the swirling current of circumstances which leaves them dazed and bewildered.

Repeatedly we hear such remarks as, "Well, I certainly don't know where we are headed," or, "There just seems to be nothing one can do to change events," or, "We seem to have lost control of our own affairs and are just drifting toward disaster," or even more emphatically, "I'd hate to be around twenty years from now!"

All of this gives expression to the deep inner dissatisfaction with life. It betrays the anxiety and gnawing worries which plague so many people. It demonstrates the dilemma and dismay of those who really wonder what life is all about. Above all it gives emphasis to the general fever of human discontent and weariness with the world.

This is a most wearing way to live. It erodes away the zest for living. It robs men and women of quiet serenity. It denies them the great calm assurance of knowing where they are going.

But once we have come into contact with Christ and recognize the great honors and privileges bestowed on us in being God's children this all changes. Probably the most astonishing alteration that takes place in our outlook is our overall attitude towards life itself and the world in general. Instead of these few years of our sojourn upon the planet earth being the great end in itself, we see it as the means to an even greater end. We discover that life is for learning, learning how better to love God and love our fellow men and love all that is worthwhile in the world.

Actually this learning to love is just another way of saying we are here to learn how to really live as our Father wishes us to live—not for self and selfish reasons, but for others, for God, and for causes much greater than ourselves. Only the person who gives his life to something or someone much greater than his own small self can ever sense the surge of God's Spirit sweeping into his spirit, catching him up in the great, eternal, ongoing purposes of God Himself.

We simply have to remember that though men and nations may be bewildered, bored, and weary with world events,

God our Father is not. Despite all the circumstances which may appear contrary to His ideals, He is still very much in control of human history. He knows precisely what He is doing with His planet and the people on it. His purposes are being fulfilled and realized down to the most minute detail.

In view of this it is downright exciting for His dear children to have a part in seeing all His program accomplished. We become actively engaged in His activities. We see ourselves playing a part that is both helpful and constructive amid a society which is otherwise chaotic and destructive. Instead of standing on the sidelines we sense that we are very much in the stream of events, so to speak. We see ourselves making a worthwhile contribution of enduring consequence in God's overall strategy.

This immediately gives positive direction to our living. It lends special significance to what we do, no matter how trivial our little common round may be. Because we are tied into and linked up with the mighty purposes of God, even our most mundane affairs take on rich meaning. All of this contributes great contentment to our individual days. Life is not just a waste of time now, but a use of time for a great cause.

This is why the beloved Brother Lawrence could write in his memoirs that it was possible for him to even pick up a straw from the ground or do dishes in the drab kitchen and do it for God his Father. The most trivial task can thus take on a touch of eternal worth.

Learning to live this way and to love this way is really a matter of maturing and growing up in God's family. Gradually as we go on there steal over us subtle but splendid changes in character. We may not be aware of these alterations ourselves, but others around us are.

What is actually happening to us is that we are gradually being conformed to the character and likeness of Christ. As we invite His Spirit to come into our careers and into our lives we find that He there tends to produce His own characteristics in us. Instead of being tense and anxious and nervous we become more calm, confident, and relaxed. This is because we become increasingly aware that just as God our Father is very much in control of outer events in the world around us, He can likewise be in calm control of the inner turmoil of the world within us.

Essentially this is what we mean by allowing ourselves to be led or guided by God. It is what we refer to as being under Christ's control. It is the thought of my spirit's being so in harmony with God's Spirit that there are a desire and willingness to do God's will.

This really is not half as mysterious or mystical as it may sound. Knowing and doing the will of God baffle a lot of well-intentioned people. They are very happy to become God's children. They are delighted to find their misconduct forgiven. They are often very happy to sense the joy of God's companionship and are more than ready to help His cause along, but, and it is a big "but," doing His will, that's different.

I feel it is very significant that the degree of contentment apparent in most lives is directly proportional to the degree in which they are doing God's will. It is akin to the old saying that "our own happiness is exactly proportional to our helpfulness."

The person who senses deep down inside that he is living and moving and acting in accord with the wishes of his heavenly Father has found the secret to sublime and serene life. He has stepped out of the swamp and quagmire of confused experiences onto the high road of solid and straightforward walking with God.

Now life is no longer an enigma. It is the way home. This world is not the last word. It is but a part of the path that prepares me for a much wider realm of life to come. Even death is not to be dreaded. It is but the doorway through which I step into a new dimension of living.

If we pause briefly to examine Christ's life on earth, we will readily see all of these attitudes in His outlook. From the beginning to the end Jesus continually emphasized and reemphasized that He was here doing His Father's will, saying what He would say, working in the way He would work. Always He reiterated and held before Himself the great joy and anticipation of going home. It is moving to study Christ's life and note how often He spoke of going to His Father. With all this in view, it is little wonder He could face Calvary and death with fortitude. Beyond the grave He knew there lay the incredible and wonderful realm of a still wider life. So, though His outer circumstances may have been tempestuous, His inner life was supremely content.

Because Jesus Christ lived and moved always in accord with the will of His Father, we see Him striding across the pages of history with a strength and dignity and purpose unmatched by any other character. Because His spirit was in harmony with the Spirit of God, we see Him achieving every aim and accomplishing every purpose for which He came to earth. In spite of what seemed utter disaster and defeat to His contemporaries, He emerges ultimately as the greatest victor over evil for all time. Notwithstanding circumstances and surroundings which would have broken and shattered anyone else, He stands strong and supreme, a character of enormous vitality and quiet contentment. Always Christ was in control both of outer events and His own inner life.

He knew where He came from. He knew exactly why He was here and what He was to do. He knew where He was going. And this being so, nothing could shake Him; nothing could deter Him from doing His Father's will; nothing could diminish His desire to achieve all that He had been sent to do.

It is, of course, possible to protest that Christ could do all this because He was divine. May I point out here in all solemnity that no man, no woman, whose spirit has been entered by the Spirit of God is any less empowered. This is not to minimize the majesty or person of Christ. It is but to affirm what He Himself declared, that those to whom His Father sent His Spirit would live as He did and achieve what He did.

A careful and unbiased reading of John's Gospel will make this clear. It is far better for the reader to discover such truths for himself than that I should here embark on a doctrinal discourse.

I have deliberately developed this theme on doing God's will simply because when all else is said and done it lies at the very heart of quiet, contented living. It is basically God's intended way of my taking life. It is what Jesus had in mind when He invited worn and tense people to come to Him and find rest. When He told them, "Take my yoke upon you and learn of me," He was not intimating that He was going to add to their burdens and make the going still tougher. What He was saying in so many words was simply this: "I know the secret to successful, contented living. I know how to take life with its tangles and its strains and its tensions. The way I have learned to handle this load that breaks men down can be passed on to you. Just come to me and I'll teach you; I'll show you the secret."

And this secret is to do His Father's will. It is to live in harmony with His Spirit. It is to be caught up and carried along in the great surging current of God's plans and purposes (His will) that flow from eternity to eternity.

To do God's will is to become an integral part of the infinite. It is to be literally incorporated into the divine ongoings of God. It is to become more than just a partner in God's eternal enterprises, but rather to be His Son; to be a member of His family; to be one in the family fortunes of God.

Paul, with his magnificent intellect and enormous spiritual perception, saw into this sublime secret. He points out in various letters to the early churches that the great honor bestowed upon God's children is that of becoming heirs and joint heirs with Jesus Christ in sharing all of the prosperity and privileges of God Himself.

This is heady stuff for us mere mortals to assimilate. It is almost intoxicating to our spirits to contemplate it. We are told not to be drunk with wine but filled with the Spirit of God. And when the full awareness of our heritage as God's children comes home to us, it is bound to make an enormous and irrevocable impact upon us.

For one thing, it is sure to shake us loose somewhat from our adherence to and reliance upon this world for either our comfort or contentment. There begins to creep over our deep inner consciousness the conviction that we really are no longer merely citizens of a country on earth, but much more, truly permanent citizens of a heavenly community. We begin to see much more clearly that we are really just passing through this earthly scene. We start to realize that all that has to do with the world is transient, temporary, and subject to deterioration or decay.

Because of all this we find our contentment, our serenity, our inner strength are no longer dependent on nor conditioned by contemporary events or materialistic values. Rather our quiet hope, confidence, and rest are centered in God and in simply identifying ourselves with Him and His aims.

This is to find serenity in harmony with His Spirit, to find contentment in complying with His wishes (commands). It also adds enormous adventure to everyday living, for each day brings me nearer home.

Before leaving this thought of doing God's will and being in harmony with Him, I should emphasize that this does not imply drifting through life. There is too often a tendency for us to become almost fatalistic about our faith in God and His great purposes. We are sometimes both lazy and apathetic about the whole issue. We shrug our shoulders and murmur sweet nothings—"What will be, will be."

This is not our Father's intention for us at all. We were granted free wills with the privilege of exercising them. And it is expected of us that we shall deliberately set ourselves to seek out and cooperate with God and His plans. We are to acquaint ourselves with His desires and, knowing them, we will presumably be determined in our efforts to comply with them. This cooperative enterprise between us and God becomes of primary importance in all of our thinking and acting and living. It conditions our attitudes and governs our actions. It is applied to every part of life. It has to do with everything that has been written in this book. It dominates every area of our body, mind, and spirits.

To live this way, really, is to live under God's guidance and control—not as a robot, but as an active, intelligent, cooperative member of His family. But to do this does not entail drabness or drudgery, as so many suspect. Quite the opposite. It sets one free to live in a rich and fully satisfying way. For one thing, it sets us free from always fretting over the future.

The unknown is in our Father's hands, and our part is simply to do what needs to be done today with lighthearted good cheer.

For another thing, there sweeps into our spirits the overwhelming assurance that nothing happens to us by coincidence or chance. We are not the mere playthings of whimsy. We are God's children, living in cooperation with Him, controlled by His wisdom and love, the objects of His unending care and deep affection.

It would not surprise me if many who read this will be extremely skeptical about it. They will question whether it is really possible for a person to live this way. To all such I say that it is. One who has learned to know and love God, who delights in cooperating with Him, has come into the position of positive and purposeful living. A tremendous sense of contentment, well-being, and relaxation from the fret of life enfolds that person.

Now it matters not whether poverty or prosperity, sickness or health, peace or war, laughter or weeping, loneliness or popularity, failure or success, make up the warp and woof of life. Behind every thread in the tapestry of our days one senses the gentle hand of our heavenly Father fashioning a pattern of unique worth and beauty.

In this calm assurance lies great peace. We are able to accept every adversity with equanimity. We are able to enjoy every triumph and delight with dignity. Gone from our lives are the tension, the stress, the strain of the old struggle to survive. In its place there is the gentle joy of contented living, the ability to be grateful for *every* event that comes to us as God's children. This is what Jesus referred to as living life more abundantly . . . at the highest level.

21

Help for the Higher Life

Anyone who has read this far is bound to ask, if he does not already know, "Where can one get help for the kind of living outlined? Is there any source to which one can turn in order to know God better, to understand His will and how to cooperate with Him?"

These are legitimate questions. And this book would not be complete without giving at least some general directions on how to know God's will and how to do it.

The first and by far the most valuable guidebook is the Bible. All through the preceding chapters, whenever I have referred to the Scriptures, I have had only the contents of the Old and New Testaments of the Bible in mind. This is a collection of sixty-six books written by some forty-odd authors over a span of history of well over 1,500 years.

I do not debate the fact that Moslems, Hindus, and Buddhists, as well as many other religions and human philosophies, have their scriptures as well. The basic difference between the Bible and other teachings is that their founders and teachers have all been mortal men, whereas the central figure of the Bible, Jesus Christ, is more than a mortal. He is the living God, active even now in our affairs. He is approachable and He reveals Himself to seeking men, and reveals His Father's wishes, by His Spirit.

Beyond this I would add only one other observation. It is this, that though I have lived and traveled widely in parts of the world dominated by other religions, there was little or no evidence that their adherents had found the secret to serene living. If anything they were more burdened by their beliefs than if they had had none at all. Nor did their scriptures seem to induce any uplifting change in their personal code of conduct. For these reasons their teachings cannot be accepted as timeless truth.

It may be argued that many so-called Christians are no different. This is readily admitted. It is an accepted fact, as stated emphatically by Christ Himself, that few would ever really know Him, that few would find this way of lofty living. But the sincere, seeking person can meet Christ. By His teachings and through His Spirit the entire tone of life can be altered from one of tension and turmoil to one of great tranquility and nobility.

Therefore, the ultimate source of spiritual enlightenment lies in the main body of the biblical Scriptures. It requires a certain amount of time and concentration and persistent reading to grasp the full impact of what has been written there. One of the rather amazing discoveries one soon makes is that the same portion may be read again and again, each time with new delight and fresh meaning. No other material ever written has this immense depth of truth to it.

It is very important to come to the Scriptures with an open mind. There are some parts which may well prove very offensive and others which can be boring. Only time will show why they have been incorporated into the collection of material. Because of this, I urge seeking hearts to begin with the New Testament and concentrate especially on the Four Gospels with their account of the life, death, resurrection, and teachings of Jesus Christ. After this move on into Acts and the Epistles. Later on one will derive great help from the

Psalms, Proverbs, and the historical books of the Old Testament.

Before beginning to read the Scriptures it is beneficial to request God to enlarge one's spiritual perception of them as one reads. This He will do by His Spirit. It is the surest way to understand both what is being read and how to apply it to our lives.

Casual and routine reading of the Bible is really of very little value. We have to be in earnest with God if we are to get to know Him and know what His wishes are. He is not much impressed by people who treat Him rather casually with a "take it or leave it" attitude.

On the other hand, when one is extremely serious about delving into the Scriptures it is remarkable how they do indeed come alive. They become very gripping and fascinating. Their truth proves to be inexhaustible and provides enormous pleasure and satisfaction to the spirit.

As one reads, it is an excellent practice to have a notebook in which one jots down the main impressions conveyed to his heart by the Spirit of God. This is one way in which God is able to speak to us not only about Himself but also about His wishes. Steadily and surely in this way there will grow upon us an increasing confidence in both God and what He says. The Scriptures will become our final terms of reference. This is a tremendously important factor in living, if for no other reason than that it eliminates much of the anxiety about what is right and what is wrong. It is not popular in our permissive society to say unequivocally, "This is decent, that is disgusting." But because so few do say it, or even know how to differentiate between the two, we live in a society smothering itself in a gray fog of frustration and confusion.

Instinctively people do want to decide and know what is proper and helpful and what is not. But because most of them never bother to read the Bible they have no final terms of reference for their conduct, so that anything goes. The net result has been to create a climate of confusion and chaos in social behavior that leaves people baffled and bewildered.

It is not easy to live under this sort of strain and anxiety. It is not surprising to find young people turn in almost every direction looking for someone or something to establish a code of conduct by which they can live in confidence and dignity. In many cases they turn to the sort of creeds and philosophies which betray their better selves, and they end up feeling very cheated and even more unsure of themselves than before.

Perhaps a brief experience I had with a very brilliant engineer will help convey what I mean. He was an extremely handsome man, tall, well-built, and very successful in his chosen field as a consulting forest engineer. He owned a beautiful home in a large city and was married to an attractive woman. They had several very brilliant children. All of his life seemed a success. But it really wasn't. Deep down inside, this man was ill at ease and discontented with life.

He came to see me one warm summer evening. We sat out on a back patio, chatting until dark. After he had unburdened himself and told his tale of discontent, we sat quietly and said little.

Then I turned to him and said, "Really, what you are looking for in life is a final frame of reference. You are an engineer. You know that in Ottawa or Washington or London there is a bureau of standards set up. There is an exact inch, an exact foot, an exact pound, an exact measurement made for everything. So when you speak of a foot or pound or inch to another person anywhere in the world, be it New York, Hong Kong, or London, he knows precisely what you mean."

. He nodded his head quietly and agreed.

"If it wasn't this way," I went on, "you engineers and the whole world would be in utter chaos. Can you imagine the terrible confusion and frustration if every engineer decided to establish his own set of standards?"

He laughed—but it was a laugh of recognition, for he already saw the point I was going to make.

"So it is with God and us. Somebody has had to set down a specific and final standard whereby we can live. He has done this for us in the Scriptures. There lie our final terms of reference. We can't possibly go wrong if we turn to the standards of the Bible and rely on them for our personal conduct."

He saw the significance of my statement. It was the turning point in his life. From then on knowing God and doing His will became to him the most important things in all the world. What is even more, frustration and misgivings soon were replaced by a deep, settled serenity in his life. Why? Because he knew he could bank on the Bible.

His personal conflicts and anxieties about his conduct were resolved. His responsibilities in rearing his family and dealing with clients were clarified. In short, he had moved from an area of uncertainty and apprehension to one of calm and quiet confidence. Now he was a man at ease with himself, at peace with his family, and relaxed in his work. This is what responding to the Word of God had done for him as an individual.

Just reading the Bible is in itself not enough. Of necessity one must comply with its instructions and cooperate in carrying out our heavenly Father's wishes. I say this is necessary simply because this is *the secret to knowing God's will*. And naturally it is essential to know God's will before one can do it. We find that as we carry out the instructions of God laid down in the Scriptures many of our more formidable difficulties are resolved.

Many people are puzzled and perplexed by what I have just said. They insist that even though they may know what God's will is, they simply do not have the ability to comply and carry it out. They assert that the standards of personal conduct set before us in Scripture are quite beyond their power to perform.

In part this is true. For so long as we stand on the sidelines, so to speak, and merely shake our heads in despair at what God asks us to do, nothing happens. On the other hand, the moment we move out of our lethargy, and in faith actually *do* what we are told to do, we discover that it is possible. This is because God, by His own Spirit, enters our spirits in response to our confidence in Him and energizes us beyond our own ability. This is precisely what Paul meant when he wrote to the Philippian church, "For it is God himself whose power creates within you both the desire and the power to execute his gracious will" (Philippians 2:13).

Even more encouraging is the fact that as we go on in this way we find it is not a struggle or a strain to do God's will, but a pleasure. There are too many people who consider this kind of life a sort of penance. They look on it with great misgivings. They feel sure they might be expected to do something desperately difficult. They are afraid it will deprive them of a certain degree of freedom and enjoyment.

The only answer I can give to such misgivings is something like the statement of the ancient psalmist, "Oh, taste and see that the Lord is good!" (Psalm 34:8). One has to try it before he can talk intelligently about it. Those who have a deep inner desire to do God's will, who are prepared to cooperate in carrying it out, soon find a freedom and joy in living they never knew before.

For many who move into this realm of loftier living there is an acute awareness that their little lives have at last been linked to the majestic and eternal purposes of God. Where before their days were but a tedious, tension-ridden existence in which they stumbled from one dilemma to another, now they sense that they are moving strongly in harmony with the infinite. There is purpose and direction to their decisions and their actions. Even the dark days and difficult times are seen not as disasters, but as disciplines that lead them to greater goals.

What is actually happening in all of this is that God our Father, by His own Spirit, is making real in us the life of the living Christ. The energy, the attitudes, the thoughts, the character of Christ are actually transmitted to our spirits and minds in such a manner that it is both possible and practical for us to live as He did. This means that even amid the most trying or tormenting circumstances of life we can live as He did in quiet strength and contented serenity.

We are bound to encounter troubles and difficulties of all sorts. We cannot hope to escape the tensions, worries, and stress of modern living. They are, as pointed out at the beginning of this book, exerting their tyranny at every turn. But we do not have to be broken and beaten by them. We can rise above them and surmount their assaults by virtue of the life and strength of God's Spirit within us.

"Greater is he that is in you than he that is in the world," reads I John 4:4. And note the words of Jesus Himself: "In this world you will have trouble. But be of good cheer! I have overcome the world!" (John 16:33). And so can you.

Very often people who read a book of this sort approach the end of it with a certain kind of apprehension. All along they had hoped the next paragraph or the next page might contain some special secret that would unlock all the mystery of life to them. Or they hoped for a single key to open wide the door to better living.

I cannot offer any such single solution. All that has been written in these pages is something like giving away a whole ring of keys. Each can unlock a different door to a separate area of life. It is as though I have tried to share fully all the secrets I own to all the rooms of life. Quite frankly I can say I have held back nothing. My main motivation in this work has been to try to help others to tame the tyranny of their tensions.

The longer I live, the more keenly I am aware that basically all that counts in life is what we can contribute of comfort, cheer, and inspiration to others. The success of our living is measured not by what we can accumulate for ourselves, but by what we can bestow upon our fellow travelers on life's tough trail.

In my wallet I have carried a small newspaper clipping for many years. I do not have any idea who the author is, nor where it came from, but I pass on these few lines as a finale to this book.

> To laugh often and much; to win the respect of intelligent people and the affection of children; to earn the appreciation of honest critics and endure the betrayal of false friends; to appreciate beauty; to find the best in others; to leave the world a bit better, whether by a healthy child, a garden patch or a redeemed social condition; to know even one life has breathed easier because you lived. This is to have succeeded.

My most earnest hope and wish is that this book will, in a practical and happy way, help many to breathe much more easily because it was written.